EXTREME
SNOWBOARDING

SO-CFJ-945

Massimiliano Angeli • Paolo Codeluppi
Stefano Martignoni • Luciana Rota

◆

EXTREME SNOWBOARDING

HISTORY, TECHNIQUE, RUNS

UNIVERSE PUBLISHING

Contents

Snow surfing

The history of modern snowboarding dates back only to the early 1960s, when an inventive skier, Sherman Poppen, dreamed up the "Snurfer". That same year, Tom Sims made something he called a "snowboard." Neither were very successful, though the Snurfer had quite a following. The first Snurfer races were held in 1968; almost ten years later, Jake Burton, a passionate East Coast skier and wannabe surfer brought a new and revolutionary prototype to the races. He had to race – alone – in a new class created just for his board. In 1977 Burton started his now-famous snowboard company. Thanks to the use of more sophisticated materials and to the introduction of steel edges and more dependable bindings, the new equipment spawned a new sport and began to attract the attention of American skiers. In the mid-1980s, snowboarding really took root in the U.S., and was soon becoming popular in Europe. Its evolution there was quick and significant. In the Alps, remarkable technological and commercial progress was made, and the first European races were organized.

THE ORIGINS
The origins of snowboarding are still wrapped in some mystery. Legend has it that in the 1920s a man slid down a mountainside in the Alps standing up on a strange contraption. Forty years later the first snurfer and windsurf boards began to appear.

THE FIRST SNOWBOARDS
There was only a slight difference between the first snowboards and Snurfer boards. The original blue version with the word Burton written in red was fairly flexible. 350 boards were made and sold for eighty-eight dollars each. Other snowboard pioneers were Milovich who, among other things, invented the first board that would bend (it cost $ 225) and Tom Sims, skateboard maker and winner of the first World Cup in Colorado in 1981 with his steel-edged boards.

The first Olympics

1998 was a historic year for snowboarding; it became an official Olympic sport, at the Winter Olympics in Nagano, Japan. The men's slalom gold went to the Canadian Ross Rebagliati. In the Half-Pipe there were surprise wins by the Swiss Gian Simmen and the German Nicola Thost. But the best snowboarders in the world were missing...

GAMES YES, BUT NOT FOR EVERYONE

Snowboarding developed very rapidly through the 80s and 90s, and along with it, competitions, from the World Cup to the Winter Olympics. But everything did not go smoothly in Nagano: many famous riders withdrew, among them the great Norwegian Terje Haakonsen. Why? They pointed to debatable rules, problems with the International Olympic Games Committee, and a basic dissatisfaction with the idea of the Olympics. Their positions were supported by their sponsors.

10,000 AT NAGANO

In spite of their criticisms, snowboarding's first Olympic appearance was highly successful. More than 10,000 spectators at Kanbayashi Snowboard Pari in Japan enjoyed what was described as the most spectacular event at the Nagano games. There were two competitions: the Giant Slalom and the Half-Pipe. In the first, gold medals went to Ross Rebagliati of Canada and Karine Ruby of France. The Half-Pipe was won by the Swiss Gian Simmen and the German Nicola Thost.

Olympics

Some of the world's strongest snowboarders boycotted the sport's first Olympics.

The best snowboarder in the world, the Norwegian Terje Haakonsen, did not participate. Twice the winner of the World Cup, Terje had beaten all the potential Olympic winners in events not directly connected to the Olympic organization. And Terje had beaten all the top American riders, including Todd Richards and Ross Powers, as well as the Norwegian Daniel Franck in the Half-Pipe. Terje was the first to withdraw, citing "power plays" within the International Olympic Committee (IOC).

Both Richards and Franck later said that a victory at Nagano without Terje could never have been a real victory.

The position of the International Olympic Committee was controversial from the moment it announced that snowboarding would be included in the 1998 Olympics. Many riders were against the presence of snowboarding at Nagano, because in their opinion the Committee was only using the sport to bring novelty to the Winter Olympic Games, which had become less popular in recent years.

GIANT SLALOM - WOMEN

1	KARINE RUBY	FRANCE
2	HEIDI REINOTH	GERMANY
3	BRIGITTE KOECK	AUSTRIA
4	LIDIA TRETTEL	ITALY
5	URSULA FINGERLOS	AUSTRIA
6	MARION POSCH	ITALY
7	DAGMAR MAIR UNTER DER EGGEN	ITALY
8	ISABELL ZEDLACHER	AUSTRIA
9	SANDRA FARMAND	ITALY
10	MARIE BIRKL	SWEDEN

HALF-PIPE - WOMEN

1	NICOLA THOST	GERMANY
2	STINE BRUN KJELDAAS	NORWAY
3	SHANNON DUNN	USA
4	CARA-BETH BURNSIDE	USA
5	MAELLE RICKER	CANADA
6	MINNA HESSO	FINLAND
7	JENNY JONSSON	SWEDEN
8	JENNIE WAARA	SWEDEN

GIANT SLALOM - MEN

1	ROSS REBAGLIATI	CANADA
2	THOMAS PRUGGER	ITALY
3	UELI KESTENHOLZ	SWITZERLAND
4	DIETER KRASSNIG	AUSTRIA
5	MATTHIEU BOZZETTO	FRANCE
6	CHRIS KLUG	USA
7	MARTIN FREINADEMETZ	AUSTRIA
8	MAXENCE IDESHEIM	FRANCE

HALF-PIPE - MEN

1	GIAN SIMMEN	SWITZERLAND
2	DANIEL FRANCK	NORWAY
3	ROSS POWERS	USA
4	FABIEN ROHRER	SWITZERLAND
5	GUILLAUME CHASTAGNOL	FRANCE
6	JACOB SODERQVIST	SWEDEN
7	SEBASTIAN KUHLBERG	FINLAND
8	MICHAEL MICHALCHUK	CANADA
9	BRETT CARPENTIER	CANADA
10	JONATHAN COLLOMB-PATTON	FRANCE

The board

There are many, many snow-boards on the market and it is not always easy to choose the right one.

It is therefore important to have some basic technical knowl-edge in order to buy the right board.

TOTAL LENGTH
The distance between the nose and tail, measured along the base.

EFFECTIVE EDGE
Distance separating the two points which the board comes in contact with when placed on its edge. The longer the edge, the greater its stability at speed and its grip in curves.

NOSE LENGTH
Distance from the tip of the nose to the point at which the board touches the snow.

TAIL LENGTH
The same measurement, but from the tail.

NOSE RADIUS
The radius of the circle inscribed in the shape of the nose.

TAIL RADIUS
The radius of the circle inscribed in the shape of the tail. Broad, high noses and tails (wider radius) guarantee better performance (floating) in powder snow. Narrow, low tails and noses (smaller radius) are better on packed trails.

WIDTH
Width is measured at the widest point of the nose, center, and tail. Narrow boards allow for greater speed and quick edge changes; wide boards provide greater stability and floating.

SIDECUT DEPTH
The distance from the edge of the narrowest part of the board to the line connecting the widest points of the nose and tail.

SIDECUT RADIUS
The radius of the ideal circle inscribed in the side of the board. The deeper the sidecut, the smaller the radius of the board's running curve.

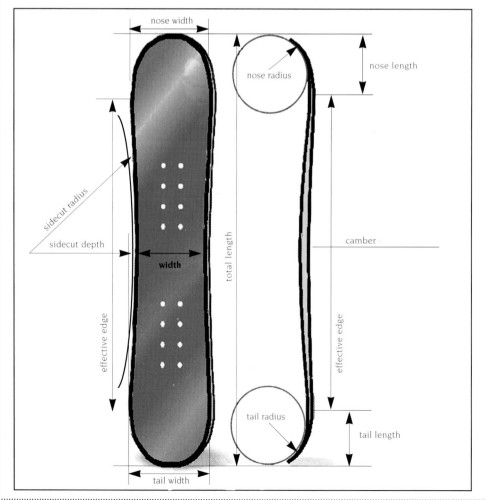

nose width

nose radius

nose length

sidecut radius

sidecut depth

width

total length

camber

effective edge

effective edge

tail radius

tail length

tail width

TORSIONAL FLEX
The force necessary to bend the board by rotating the nose and tail in opposite directions.

LONGITUDINAL FLEX
The force necessary to bend the board lengthwise. Rigid boards allow for more controlled turns, even at high speeds, but they require more active guidance. Soft boards turn at lower speeds and allow for short-range turns.

CAMBER
The distance separating the base of the board from the flat ground; it depends on the tension of the board. It will increase or decrease when a rider stands on his or her board, depending on their weight. Greater camber makes the board more stable at speed, while less camber renders the board more maneuverable.

SHAPE
- Symmetrical: when the sidecuts are identical.
- Asymmetrical: when the sidecuts differ and are off axis.
- Directional: when the nose has different dimensions from the tail.

- Twin tip: when the nose and tail are identical.

CORE
- Wood: woods of different characteristics, qualities, and widths are assembled in a laminate structure in a vertical or horizontal arrangement. One of the most used and most recommended materials.
- Foam: a low-cost synthetic material, generally used for cheaper boards.

- Torsion Box: a fiber structure, usually fiberglass strengthening a lightweight core.

CONSTRUCTION
- Sandwich: the materials are superimposed and pressed.
- Cap: the materials are enclosed in a shell that is wrapped directly around the edges.
- Semicap: the materials integrated or superimposed, with a double sandwich and cap construction.
- Injected: the materials are injected into a preformed structure.

BASE
- Sintered: the material that makes up the base is first pulverized, then recompressed. This guarantees greater ski wax permeability.
- Extruded: a layer of polyethylene is simply pressed and united to the board.
- Graphite: graphite is added to the sintered or extruded base in order to increase slide.

EDGES
Edges are indispensable for gripping. They're assembled together with the base.

From top to bottom: three views of modern snowboard construction: sandwich (the materials are superimposed and pressed), semicap, and cap (the core is enclosed in a kind of shell, which also encloses the edges).

Types of boards

Snowboards can be divided into five categories: Freeride, Freestyle, Boardercross, Free-carve, and Race.

Boards of each category are also available for women and children, and can differ in length, width, flexibility, and weight.

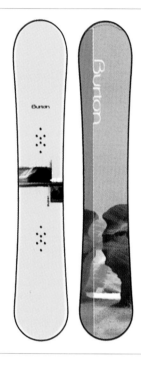

Freeride board

IDEAL DIMENSIONS
Length: 65.5 inches
Sidecut radius: 338 inches
Effective edge: 50 inches
Center width: 9.7 inches

CHARACTERISTICS

Freeride boards are long and reactive. They're ideal for riders who love to have fun both on and off the trail: they sustain speed in carving, yet offer the joy of an occasional free jump or ride in powder. They are wide enough and light enough to guarantee good floating in powder, are long, to increase the grip of the edge in turns, and they offer a greater support surface for landings, yet they are very manageable.

They are usually semirigid and are used with soft bindings, with two to three clamps, according to how reactive you want your board to be.

LONGBOARDS AND POWDER

The Freeride category includes two subcategories: Longboard (or Extreme) and Powder. Longboards are bigger and suitable for taller or heavier riders, and for those who do not want to give up downhill even in extreme conditions. The classic Powder board, on the other hand, has the traditional swallowtail which, while limiting its use on trails, guarantees great sensations in powder.

Half-Pipe boards

IDEAL DIMENSIONS
Length:
59.4 inches
Sidecut radius:
302 inches
Effective edge:
45.8 inches
Center width:
9.4 inches

Freestyle boards

IDEAL DIMENSIONS
Length:
60.8 inches
Sidecut radius:
318 inches
Effective edge:
47 inches
Center width:
9.7 inches

CHARACTERISTICS

Half-Pipe boards have shorter effective edges and raised tails. They're not for going fast, but they're perfect for descents with moguls and on soft snow.

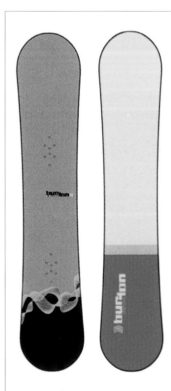

Snow Park boards

IDEAL DIMENSIONS
Length:
59.6 inches
Sidecut radius:
306.6 inches
Effective edge:
47 inches
Center width:
9.5 inches

CHARACTERISTICS

This is the ideal board for anyone who wants to try out all types of tricks, especially rotations. It must be relatively short for easy handling; wide, for good stability when landing and to allow the feet to be positioned perpendicularly to the axis; soft, to facilitate maneuvers; and as light as possible without jeopardizing sturdiness.
The preferred shape is the Twin, with identical nose and tail.
Soft bindings are mounted centrally; the distance between them (stance) is subjective, in general about 19.5-21.5 inches. Increasing the distance between bindings may be counterproductive for medium-height riders, both for performance and safety in case of falls.
The freestyle category includes two subcategories: Half-Pipe and Snow Park.

CHARACTERISTICS

Used primarily for tricks on flat terrain, and on special or improvised structures. They don't allow for fast speeds.

Boardercross boards

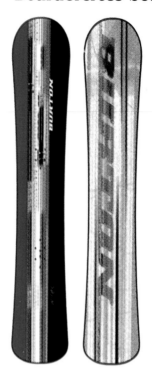

IDEAL DIMENSIONS
Length:
63 inches
Sidecut radius:
361 inches
Effective edge:
53.6 inches
Center width:
8.5 inches

CHARACTERISTICS

Designed for top performance on Boardercross runs — special tracks with turns, jumps, and bumps. The board must have a good grip on curves, be fast, and at the same time remain manageable. Either hard or soft bindings may be used.

Boardercross is the newest snowboarding discipline. Athletes compete in elimination heats on a single track, making breathtaking passes. It is very popular, and often spectacular.

Freecarve boards are usually used with rigid bindings (or sometimes three-clamp soft bindings) in order to better exploit their speed and guidance features.
Freecarve boards are perfect for people who love soft footwear and bindings. The angle of the front foot is rarely less than 30°.
The boots are hard, although less rigid than Race models, in order to give the ankle more freedom.

Freecarve boards

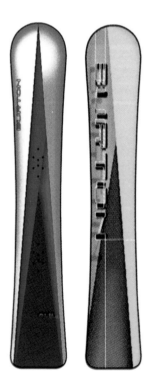

IDEAL DIMENSIONS
Length:
64 inches
Sidecut radius:
366 inches
Effective edge:
55.7 inches
Center width:
8.4 inches

CHARACTERISTICS

Ideal for having fun with packed snow, this board also allows for some wandering onto powder. It is perfect for medium and high speeds. It's narrow, permitting rapid edge changes; has rigid flexibility, for immediate response; and it has a long effective edge, for better control in turns.

RACE STRATEGY

It is more important in Boardercross than in any other discipline to establish a race strategy. Observe your adversaries carefully, and study the run in advance.
This way, you can determine if you need to attack from the very beginning.

In some cases a "wait" strategy may be advantageous, especially if your opponents are too impetuous and crowd into tricky narrow passages. Learn to exploit the mistakes of others in order to pass them at the right moment.

Try not to prolong your jump – the more time you spend in the air the more speed you lose. You must be in perfect control when you land in order to be ready for the next obstacle.

Giant Slalom boards have been designed for high speeds and wide turns. This kind of performance demands broader curving (that is, less accentuated sidecuts) and longer effective edges.
The boards are symmetrical, rather rigid, prestressed, and very stable.

Race boards

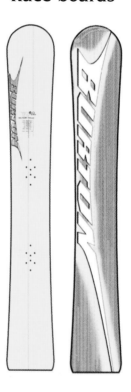

CHARACTERISTICS

If you want to reach high speeds and push your capabilities to their limits in races, this is the ideal board. But Race boards require special attention and tender loving care to keep them at their best. In general, they're about 7-7.8 inches wide. A wider board guarantees greater stability and support, while a narrower one offers greater speed when you're changing edges. Race boards have elevated edge grips which can attack harder and icier snow and reach greater speeds, even on steep slopes.

IDEAL DIMENSIONS
Length:
62.4 inches
Sidecut radius:
378 inches
Effective edge:
55.3 inches
Center width:
7.8 inches

The Slalom board is shorter and more reactive than the Giant Slalom and has a more accentuated sidecut. It's designed to offer maximum manageability, edge grip, and quick edge changes, all of which are indispensable for descent through the poles. They can be symmetrical or asymmetrical.

How to choose bindings

Bindings are divided into hard and soft categories, depending on the type of boots used. The trend is to use lighter and more durable materials for both types, without sacrificing comfort. Most bindings are fastened to the board by four screws (the holes form a 1.5 inch square), but there are other systems, such as the 3D. Make sure that your board and bindings are compatible. The latest advance is the Step-in system, a hard or soft binding with an automatic release similar to that used on skis — except that they do not automatically release. It is no longer necessary to sit on the snow and use your hands!

Hard (or Plate) bindings

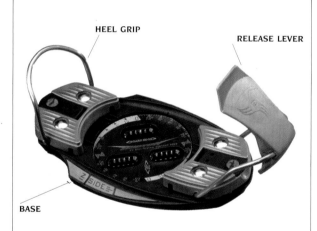

HEEL GRIP

RELEASE LEVER

BASE

Hard bindings are used with rigid boots – in some aspects similar to ski boots – on Race and Freecarve boards. They may be of aluminum, steel, plastic resins, carbon, Kevlar, or titanium. Rather than clamps, they have a simple release lever. In order to find the perfect center of the board, they usually have a lateral inclination and a "Lifting" to optimize front inclination. The heel of the boot must be firmly set into the heel grip and the front lever must close easily and perfectly over the tip. Both binders can be regulated with respect to the center, in order to fit different size boots.

Soft (or Shell) bindings

CLAMP

ADJUSTMENT INCLINATION

BASE

GRADUATED DISK

Used with soft boots, these bindings are mounted on Freestyle and Freeride boards. Traditional models have two clamps, but there are also three-clamp models equipped with a higher and wider back. These are preferable for freeriding if greater board control is desired. Backs come in different heights (high, medium, low), and the front inclination is adjustable in order to optimize response to movement.

There are also soft bindings without bases, where the boot comes in contact with the board, to provide the sensitivity and feedback required by Freestyle boards.

How to choose boots

Boots are also divided into hard and soft. Freecarvers and racers opt for the former because they are more efficient in transmitting movements to the board. The latter, very sensitive and reactive, are indispensable for Freestyle tricks, but are also a good choice for Freeriding.

Hard boots

These boots are ideal for those who want maximum precision and the immediate transmission of movements to the board. They are a must for racing and carving. While early models originated in part from skiing, today's boots have vibration deadening systems, perfect binding compatibility, micrometric release levers, and maximum foot retention. There are two types of outer shell: front-opening with an outside tongue, or with two flaps that are superimposed over the front. Athletes prefer thermoformable boots that adapt perfectly to the foot,

increasing guidance precision, with polyamide exteriors that maintain their characteristics even with sudden temperature changes. Within this category, riders can choose between the Freecarving models, with two-clamp fasteners, for lightweight people and beginners, and three clamps, which do not block the foot too much. Race models, with four clamps, rigid even at lateral tensions, are equipped with adjustments that not only permit angulation but also offer greater resistance when bending forward. These boots, suitable for people who require optimum support, have higher ankle coverage for better grip.

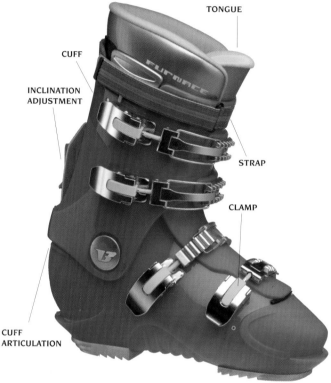

TONGUE

CUFF

INCLINATION ADJUSTMENT

STRAP

CLAMP

CUFF ARTICULATION

Hard boots are essential for alpine racing because they transmit movement immediatly to the board.

Soft boots

TONGUE

UPPER

SOLE

These boots are the most sensitive and reactive because of their remarkable flexibility and softness. But this comfort delays the transmission of movements to the board. Soft boots are used with Freestyle, Freeride, or Boardercross boards. The better models come with leather uppers (resistant, flexible, long-lasting), double – and triple – density bases, which absorb violent blows better, and treads engraved so as to guarantee optimum grip. The bases are rounded at the extremities, so they don't protrude over the edges of the board, allowing for greater bending in turns. Some soft boots have an inner shoe; this set-up is preferred by Freeriders, who desire greater support and a relatively stiff boot. Freestylers, on the other hand, prefer boots without an inner shoe in order to have maximum comfort and lightness, and a lower boot for better ankle mobility. These boots offer maximum freedom of movement, especially laterally. The tongue must be sufficiently padded to guarantee comfort at the point where it contacts the soft binding strap.

Protective gear

Snowboarding is not a particularly dangerous sport — at least no more so that any other outdoor activity. However, it is wise to take precautions, especially since protective gear lets you move faster and more safely. And it goes without saying that adequate protection is essential for anyone who races.

In the Slalom, where one frequently hits the supple poles with arms and legs, "classic" types of protection are important: shin guards, forearm guards, and protective visors.

Motocross vests have been adopted for Boardercross because there is often violent contact between racers. Helmets are not always necessary, but remember, people are not always careful, even on overcrowded ski slopes.

On the left and right: rigid back guard, jointed, integrated into the vest or fastened with an elastic waistband. This is composite plated armor made with the same technology as motocross equipment.

In the Slalom, the poles are hit with the forearm and front leg. Protection against these impacts is the same as that used by skiers, including a helmet to protect the face in the event of pole backlash.

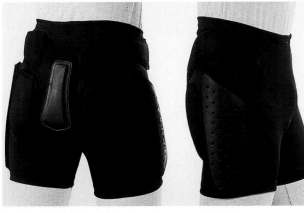

Shorts, to wear under the suit, have rigid protection over the femur and coccyx and soft protection over the pelvis, hips, and buttocks.

Clothing

You can't tell a rider by his clothes... but his clothes can certainly help him prepare for the at times extreme conditions that a passionate snowboarder might run into. That's why it is important to buy comfortable clothes that provide free movement, though it is often not easy to choose from the many specialized garments of varying quality and cost on the market.

VEST
A vest offers efficient protection from the cold and wind without quilted sleeves getting in the way.

WINDBREAKER
A good windbreaker has vents, usually zippered, wherever the body is most subject to perspiration. A heavy jacket, with a detachable hood if possible, is ideal for more difficult conditions and essential in heavy snowfalls.

PANTS
Pants must be comfortable, waterproof, and maintain the right body temperature in all weather conditions. Those with a bib and straps offer better protection and are preferred by those who like to ride in powder. It is also good to have reinforced material or built-in knee pads, since the knee area gets a lot of wear.

UNDERWEAR

Clothing under a windbreaker should be warm, lightweight, and provide good insulation. It is best to dress in layers, with underwear made of special synthetic fibers that can regulate body temperature and perspiration, so that the wind and air do not freeze perspiration on the skin.

HATS

A good hat that covers the ears ensures that heat and energy is not lost. The popular adage that it is wise to wear a hat when your feet are cold is always valid; the body should not have to pump blood to the head in order to get warm.

FLEECE

A fleece garment is ideal to wear over your underwear and under your windbreaker. There are models on the market with a windproof layer that guarantees insulation.

GLOVES

Gloves usually have robust seams and anti-abrasion palms. They should offer good insulation and allow perspiration.
The inner glove should be removable for better drying and for use in warmer temperatures. Models with laces, straps, or elastic bands on the wrist to keep out the snow are preferable, as are gloves that come up high over the jacket cuff.

Preparing the board

Preparing and waxing the bottom of a snowboard and sharpening its edges are not easy. But a well-prepared base and correctly sharpened edges will improve performance: the board will change edges more easily, it will slide more rapidly, and it will maintain better contact with the ground.

You'll find all the information you need to learn how to wax your board correctly on these pages.
First of all, make sure that the bottom is flat; if you notice that the base or the edges are high, have them straightened by a dealer. And you'll have to equip yourself with wax sticks, brushes, files, and an iron.

Before you start

First eliminate rust, snags, and scratches from the edges. To remove rust, run a pumice stone along the edges. Keep your hand steady and do not press too hard. Older rust spots will require more pressure. Repeat after sharpening the edges; be more forceful on the first 2 inches at the nose and tail ends, using delicate circular movements. A little of the edge will be removed so that the board will be more manageable on entering and exiting turns. The photo shows Sandra Farmand, German, World Cup athlete, First Overall in World Pro Tour '94

Solvent for cleaning the base

Waxing a dirty base lets dust in, so you must carefully clean the bottom before waxing.
Fix the board onto a flat surface (suction vices are readily available), apply a coat of solvent to the base, let it penetrate for a few seconds, then wipe with a clean cloth.
Use solvents made for snowboards only, so you don't ruin the bottom of the board.

Repairing the base: the wax stick

The classic wax stick is the basic material for bases. After cleaning the area that needs repair, pass a sharp knife over the damaged zone. Light the wax stick as you would a candle, keeping it far from curtains and carpets. Let the wax drip onto a metal blade until the stick stops smoking.

Keeping it a couple inches from the base, let some wax drop into the hole, filling it. Wait for it to cool completely. Scrape off the excess wax, first with a metal scraper, then with fine sandpaper.

Repairing the base: powder products

Holes can also be filled with a powder, though the procedure is not as easy as the wax stick. Cover the damaged area completely with the powder, and then with a sheet of aluminum foil. Pass an iron (on the wool or silk setting) over it for not more than 20 seconds. Wait for it to cool completely. Take off the aluminum foil and remove any excess product with a metal scraper.

Sharpening the edges

Eliminate rust and snags with a pumice stone or fine sandpaper. Then, with a specially graduated file holder, called an edge tool, make sure that the angle of the side of the edge is between 87° and 90°. An angle between 88° and 89° is advisable for carving, for icy snow you might opt for an 87° angle, for better adherence. Place the edge tool against the surface of the base and slide it along the edge, exerting moderate pressure. Repeat on the other edge, touching up the nose and tail with the pumice stone. Remember that you should always sharpen the edges from the nose to the tail. Your movements should be long and steady. The photo shows Sigi Graber, German, World Pro Tour athlete.

Warm waxing

After cleaning the base, place the bar of wax on a warm iron and let it drip onto the base. If it starts to smoke, lower the temperature of the iron. Move the iron over the wax, distributing it well until the whole surface becomes shiny. Cool, then pass a clean cloth over the surface. The photo shows K.H Zangerl, Austrian, 2nd in World Pro Tour Slalom in '93-94 and '94-95.

Waxing and brushing

It is essential to completely eliminate the excess wax and to brush the base well. After letting the wax cool, remove it with a large brush, passing over the surface from the nose to the tail. Use the edges of the brush to remove wax from the board's edges and sides.

Liquid waxes

Preparing the board with cold wax is easier and faster. It can be applied without using an iron and the board can be polished much faster. The final result is a brilliant finish that will last for many runs.

Shake the bottle of wax and distribute it evenly with a cloth (Don't use too much.) Let it dry for five minutes, then polish with a clean cloth. Never use a hair-dryer or heater for drying!

Cream waxes

Cream waxes are also easy to apply. They're ideal for last-minute operations, just before you're ready to hop onto the lift. They are also excellent for touch-ups.

Using the special applicator, apply the cream to the base with rotating movements and slight pressure. Let dry, then polish scrupulously with a clean cloth.

Cold waxing

A product with fluoro-additives suitable for all kinds of snow may be used instead of the classic wax, or as a final treatment after the normal waxing operation. Before starting, make sure that the board is clean and dry; if it isn't, dry it with a clean cloth. Start by rubbing the product along the surface of the base. Work lengthwise, with long, broad movements, making sure that there is no accumulation of wax. Finish by polishing with a soft cloth.
The photo shows Martina Magenta, Italian, World Pro Tour athlete, 2nd in Continental Championship '94-95.

There are different types of cold waxes on the market. They are usually characterized by different colors according to the types of snow they are to be used for. A board with the right wax is a sure bet for fast descents and fun on the snow.

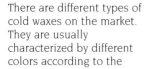

The snow

Snow can be fresh, powdery, old, windy, marbleized, icy, wet or artificial. It is important to always apply the right wax for the conditions. Before applying a wax, be sure to carefully read the instructions that came with it. Paraffin-based waxes, enriched with fluoro-components, are extremely water-repellant and prevent dirt from sticking to the bottom, guaranteeing maximum speed.

Snow crystals

FRESH SNOW
Crystals with clear edges. Provokes strong friction between the snow and the base of the board.

MARBLEIZED SNOW
The points of the crystal are rounded, though the snow remains soft.

WET SNOW
At 0° C there is water among the crystals. At lower temperatures the snow turns to ice.

OLD SNOW
The snow loses its crystalline structure.

Wax

There are many products for preparing boards. Experience acquired in the skiing world has been transferred to snowboarding, so we can use the best waxes. It is good to try different products before choosing a wax. And remember that the product by itself is not enough; correct application is essential.

Binding terminology

• **STANCE**: position of the bindings on the board. Stance width is the distance between the binding centers. Stance position is the distance between the stance center and the board center. A wide stance guarantees stability and manageability, as well as superior flexibility in response to the actions of the snowboarder. A centered stance gives balanced rotations, but lessens the grip on the heelside edge. A rear stance helps in carving on packed snow, in heelside turns, and in floating in new snow.

• **ANGLE**: the position of the bindings with respect to the long axis of the snowboard. Acute angles permit a greater stance width and better control in jumps and landings; they also increase fakie speed. Acute angles must be used on narrow boards, which require a greater transmission of power. They make carving easier.

• **CANTING**: lateral inclination (toward the center of the board) of the binding.

• **LIFTING**: the front inclination of the binding. Canting and lifting permit the knees to come close to each other; they make carving easier, and help maintain body alignment even if an accentuated-angle stance is being used.

• **T-NUTS**: inserts, fixed on the board's surface, for the binding screws.

• **GRADUATED DISK**: permits the bindings to be angled precisely.

BINDING POSITIONING

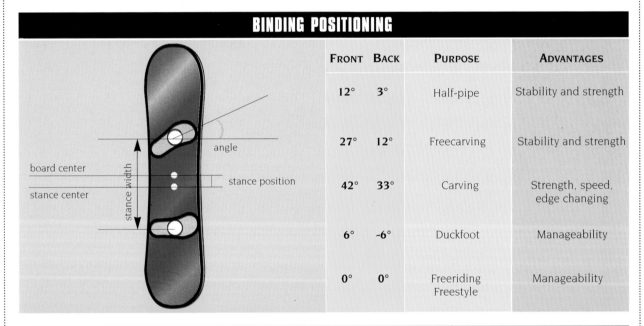

FRONT	BACK	PURPOSE	ADVANTAGES
12°	3°	Half-pipe	Stability and strength
27°	12°	Freecarving	Stability and strength
42°	33°	Carving	Strength, speed, edge changing
6°	-6°	Duckfoot	Manageability
0°	0°	Freeriding Freestyle	Manageability

TYPES OF BUCKLING

STANDARD 4x4	BURTON 3D	BURTON B4	4x4 AMPLIFIED	PRESTON '96	LAMAR '96

FREERIDING

First steps

It's possible to teach yourself how to use a snowboard, but as in any other sport, it is essential to have a good teacher if you want to learn quickly and well. In addition, filmed or videotaped sequences are very helpful in seeing one's mistakes.

Always make sure to warm up and stretch for a few minutes before starting to avoid muscle cramps. For your first attempts, choose a place that's relatively calm with a slight slope that opens onto a flat, wide area.

Basic frontside curve

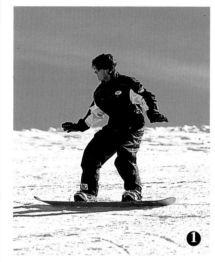

Start down the slope on a slight diagonal, keeping your knees bent.

Straighten up and shift your weight onto your front foot.

The board will level out on the snow, letting you switch to the other edge.

When you straighten up, your weight will shift to the front of your feet.

Leaning forward, your weight shifts onto the frontside edge.

Bring your weight back to the center of the board; return to a diagonal descent.

Basic backside turn

Once you have learned to make the basic frontside turn, try a backside turn — on the back, or heel edge. This may seem difficult at first; actually, it is just a matter of overcoming your natural fear of bending backwards. The time you spend learning this basic move will be more than repaid when you're able to link these two turns, one after the other. Only after you have mastered these two maneuvers should you try to go down a trail. Make sure no one is coming up behind you. Try not to exaggerate your movements. When you straighten up after bending in a turn, avoid shifting your center of gravity to the outside of the board, so you don't lose your balance. Make sure your weight moves from your toes to your heels.

❶ Head down the slope on a slight diagonal, your weight over the center of the board (see No. 6 basic frontside curve) and your legs bent.

❷ Start to straighten up. Your body and eyes should face the direction you're moving. The board should be flat on the snow and you should feel pressure on your heels.

Your weight moves from your toes to your foot and then to your heels, transferring pressure to the backside edge. Your weight should be on your front leg.

Start the turn, helping it along by bending your front knee slightly forward. Your body should always be facing the direction you're moving. Be careful not to rotate too much, you'll risk losing the tail.

Keep the pressure on your front leg constant as you start to turn, and begin to lower your center of gravity by bending your knees.

Bend your knees and ankles more as you shift onto the backside edge to finish the turn.

Move back to the center of the board and get your balance back to be ready for the next turn.

Straighten up and keep your eyes and lead arm toward the direction you're moving.

Conducted frontside curve

By conduction we mean the almost perfect adherence of the edge of the board to a curvilinear trajectory. It is the next step in learning basic turning. Having the necessary control for conducting the board perfectly means you've found your equilibrium. This is when your center of gravity is inside the board, and stays there even as you move and modify the trajectory of the turn, which changes with the terrain and the situation.

Starting from a diagonal, prepare to turn by bending your knees. Start to straighten up, angling the board on its edge. Continue the movement, maintaining the angle and pushing against the centrifugal force that pushes you to the inside

of the turn. Proceed by increasing or decreasing the bend and the angle, keeping in mind both the terrain and your speed. Try to use the entire length of the edge, and to follow a perfect curve, so you'll be able to connect to the next turn.

BRIEF SUGGESTIONS

It is essential to keep your shoulders and back straight in order to end your turns without falling or skipping. By staying low and putting greater pressure on the edge of the board, this keeps the center of gravity of your body from leaving the center of the board. It also lets your knees work better by avoiding useless hip movement.

Try to shift your body as little as possible when you move. The result will be a graceful, fluid movement. At the beginning of a turn, when your knees are bent the most, there is the greatest stress on your hips and legs.

Weight distribution is important. At the beginning of a turn, move your weight onto your front leg. At the end of it, shift it to your back leg. This will speed up the board. After finishing a turn, bring your weight back onto your front leg, moving your body upward and forward in order to be ready for the next turn.

Try to keep the upper part of your body as still as possible. Every move will make the turn more difficult. Rotating too much in the direction of the turn slows down your body's return to its initial position and prevents a quick transition into the next turn.

An excellent exercise is to hold a ski pole horizontally behind your neck while you're snowboarding. Only the lower part of your body will move and a pre-rotation will be prevented. You'll have good results after just a few tries, and your curves will seem much easier.

Never keep your knees together – your back leg will put more pressure on the edge, making turning more difficult.

Conducted backside curve

At this point the different turn techniques should no longer hold any secrets for you. So it's just a question of putting into practice what you have learned to make the conducted backside turn. But one piece

of advice: when you're doing this turn, be careful not to lean too far back as you are pushed by the increased speed of the board. You'll finally be able to leave those sharp tracks in the snow you've been dreaming about.

Exiting from a frontside turn, with your weight centered on the board, lean onto your toes (1) and get ready to straighten out, to begin changing direction (2).
By rotating your body (not too much!) and shifting your weight onto your front leg, you'll give power to the turn.
The shift of weight from the toes to the heels will flatten out the board and change your edge (3).

❶

❷

❸

The pressure is now on the backside edge, and the board has passed over the line of maximum incline. Start to bend in order to charge the edge and guide the board through the turn with precision (4-5-6-7). As usual, your body and knees should face the direction of movement.

4

5

6

7

8

In pictures 8-9, the rider has remained too "seated" and in the wrong position for too long, charging the board too much. He has lost speed, and since he didn't straighten up immediately, he's not prepared for the next turn.

9

The Vitelli Turn

This spectacular turn, also known as the Euro Carve, was named for the Frenchman Serge Vitelli, the first who managed to complete it. Here, your balance is pushed to the maximum as you exploit the  centrifugal force of the curve, practically stretching out on the snow. The best riders can curl one Vitelli Turn into another, even in small spaces, without slowing down or falling.

Without losing your balance, approach the turn rapidly (1).

Execute a prerotation of the body, keeping your hips, chest, and head facing the direction of the turn (2).

Bring your outside shoulder forward, toward your front knee (3).

Let your inside hand slide onto the snow to stabilize yourself (4).

Descent with moguls

Moguls, the fear of many riders, can be fun once you've mastered the technique. Start out on a trail that's not too difficult, with powdery snow and moguls that aren't too close to one another. You'll soon discover that it is much easier to slip between moguls than slide over them. You have to crouch more than when you're descending a trail. Bend your legs as much as you can in order to bring your center of gravity as close as possible to the snowboard. Reactivity is the key: never approach a mogul with your body and legs tense. It is very important to keep your hands and arms forward and your shoulders horizontal. Try to move your torso as little as possible, and avoid wasting energy in useless movements. Once you have chosen your mogul, approach it at a speed that lets you maintain perfect control over the board. Turn your body toward your chosen path. Ride between the moguls, exploiting the wall they have created so you can keep moving. Try not to let the board slip — slide over the moguls. When you change edges, help yourself by bending over your ankles and knees, bringing them as close as possible to your chest. Don't ever be in a rigid position. Keep your body crouched and ready to absorb any rough bumps. It is important to stay low on the snowboard and to avoid useless upper body movements, leaving your legs with the job of turning the board. Use them like a spring, to lighten the board for changes in direction, and keep pressure distributed evenly along the length of the edge.

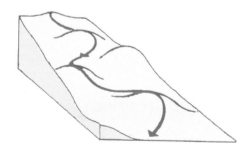

CROSSING OVER MOGULS
This technique consists of crossing right over the moguls, absorbing their impact by bending and straightening your legs in correspondence with the top and the hollow of the mogul.

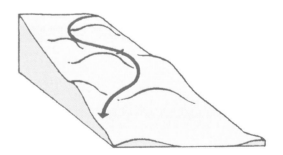

GOING AROUND MOGULS
The easiest technique for dealing with moguls exploits the natural path between them. Start off by trying to slide the board between one mogul and the next one.

Stretching

Stretching exercises are designed to lengthen and extend the muscles in order to maintain or regain body flexibility. These exercises should be started carefully and increased gradually so as not to cause strain. The series of exercises shown below should prove helpful for keeping in shape for any sport activity and, in particular, for snowboarding.

CALVES AND ANKLES

Bend one knee on the ground and place your other foot next to it. Move your body forward, raising your heel an inch or so. Using your body weight, try to put your heel down on the ground without moving. Maintain this position for 30 seconds.

INNER AND OUTER THIGH

Sit on the ground with one leg straight out in front of you. Bend your other leg and pull it toward the opposite shoulder with your hands, without moving your pelvis. Hold this position for 20-25 seconds.

CALVES AND ANKLES

With your hands on the floor, lean forward, forming an upside-down "V" with your body. Keep your knees straight and your feet flat on the floor. Stay in this position for 20 seconds.

BACK OF THE THIGH

Bend your body forward, hold onto your ankles and bend your knees slightly, bring your chest as close as possible to your knees. Hold this position for at least 40 seconds.

CALVES AND ANKLES

Stand up and lean against a wall with one foot in front of the other, both heels flat on the floor. Keep your rear leg straight at first, then bend it in order to stretch the muscle. Hold this position for 20 seconds.

FRONT OF THE THIGH

Bend your leg and prop your foot on a piece of furniture behind you. Keeping an upright position, move your upper body back. Hold this position for 25 seconds for each leg.

ELASTICITY OF ARM MUSCLES

Kneel on the ground. Keeping your back straight, take hold of your left elbow. Pull it toward the center of your back with your right hand. Hold this position for 15 seconds. Change arms and repeat.

ELASTICITY OF ARM MUSCLES

Stand up with your legs apart and your arms over your head. Pull your right arm toward the back of your neck with your body flexed toward the left. Repeat on the other side. Maintain muscle tension for 20 seconds.

POWDER

Backcountry equipment

Backcountry snowboarding can be great, but if you want to have peace of mind when you set off, you should bring safety equipment. Also, don't forget that the weather can change very suddenly in the mountains. When preparing your itinerary, it is important to keep in mind the type of snow you'll be running into and the capabilities of your companions. (Don't go off-trail alone!) Before leaving, tell someone where you're going and listen to the weather forecast. Don't leave if bad weather is expected.

TELESCOPIC POLES/PROBE

These are of great help when climbing, testing the snow before stepping on it, and probing for avalanche victims.

Light alloy or plastic poles can be carried easily in a backpack.

ANTI-AVALANCHE SHOVEL

A lightweight, collapsible shovel is essential for digging people out from under an avalanche quickly.

FIRST AID

When going off-trail, it is essential to bring these bare necessities: a thermal cover or bivouac bag for hypothermia, bandages, antiseptic gauze, and adhesive tape. You should also be familiar with the basics of first aid. Don't be caught unprepared in emergencies, when simple actions might save a life.

SKI POLES

These are the best equipment for moving on the snow. They are particularly useful on trails that are not too long and have a slight slope.

AVALANCHE DETECTOR

There are different types of detectors on the market, but they all have the same function: they emit radio signals. They have two modes: a transmitter when others are searching for you and a receiver when you are searching for others. Make sure your detector is working properly before going off on any excursion; make sure the batteries are charged and check that it's on "receive." Every member of the group should always carry one.

CRAMPONS

These are necessary when faced with very steep slopes, on mixed foundations of rock and snow, and on very hard-packed snow.

TOUR BOARDS

A special board that can be divided in half and attached like skis, thanks to special bindings. They can also be covered with sealskin to climb slopes more easily. They are very useful for excursions with long climbs, but aren't as good for descents.

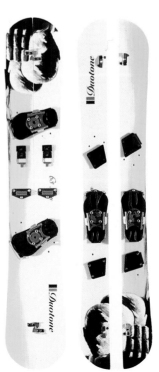

BACKPACK

Your backpack should be comfortable and big enough to carry all the necessary items, including the board, and it should have adjustable hip and shoulder straps to distribute weight. Some models have openings in the middle for easier access to the lower layers.

Backcountry snowboarding

Riding freely on powder offers unique and priceless sensations. But it is essential to know how to recognize and avoid the dangers of the mountains. First, never set off into the backcountry on your own. Always have a friend or local guide accompany you. Snow hides crevasses and rocks, and thick deposits of it can start to slide simply by passing over them, sometimes only a few yards from a marked trail. Pay attention to the weather forecast and bring suitable clothing and equipment. Also, bring an avalanche detector.

Useful advice for the backcountry

Some simple rules dictated by common sense and by those who have learned to respect the mountains:

• Regardless of your physical preparation and ability, never venture off-trail alone.
• Listen to the weather forecast and the avalanche bulletin before any excursion. If you are already on the trail and the weather looks sketchy, head back.
• Always bring safety equipment: an avalanche detector, probe, shovel, first-aid kit, and a bivouac bag or thermal cover. Check out your avalanche detector and radio before setting out.
• Make sure everyone knows how to use the safety equipment by having practical demonstrations.
• Wear functional clothing only (good underwear, a hat, warm sweaters, gloves), and don't forget your sunglasses, sunscreen, watch, compass, and altimeter. Bring food for longer excursions.
• Test all your safety equipment in a calm place. Know how to use them in case of emergency.
• Always tell someone – the hotel or resort or a friend – what itinerary you plan to follow. Rescuers will be able to reach you as quickly as possible.
• Always watch out for members of your group who are less experienced or who have become tired. They are at greater risk. Have them stay in front of the pack, so you can help them if they get into trouble.

NEW SNOW

New snow means jumps,
life, shouts, dreams, ecstasy.
There is really no special
technique for powder snow.
One piece of advice:
narrow-nosed boards
risk sinking into the snow;
broad-nosed ones are true
floaters. If you can, attach
your bindings as far back
as possible to the board.
The nose will stay out
of the snow and you're
sure to have a good time.
Keep a broad stance so
you will feel safer and
steadier. Longer boards
are also better in powder.

Cliff jump

To jump off a snowy peak into empty space unleashes a charge of adrenaline — not only in those who have the guts to do it, but also in those who are lucky enough to see it. Obviously, there are many risks involved. Like a diver, the rider who is about to jump off a peak should check his landing point carefully. Snow can hide rocks and other dangers. The landing area should be sloping, so that you avoid a painful flat landing. Try to jump from a point that immediately projects you away from the cliff. Excellent athletic preparation and total board control, in flight as well as on the ground, are indispensable for avoiding accidents. Remember that you must always proceed by degrees and never try anything that is beyond your abilities.

TACKLING THE BIG JUMP

After checking your jump-off and landing points, calmly hook yourself onto your board. Concentrate on what you are about to do. Visualize the different stages of the jump.
Only when you feel sure of yourself and are completely relaxed should you approach the edge (1), acquiring the speed necessary to be launched as far as possible from the cliff (2-3-4).
Once you're in flight, stay crouched and composed and avoid any fluttering your arms and legs, which might make you lose your balance (5-6-7-8).
The first times you jump, don't try to do any tricks. Concentrate on the basic movements. Tricks will come in time; for the moment, don't let them distract you. Cushion the impact of landing with your legs (called "stomping the landing") and let the board run down the slope, to reduce the chance of a fall (9-10). Landing after a difficult jump like this one necessitates a good amount of soft snow. Don't be tempted by jumps that are beyond your ability. Before you try a cliff jump, watch good riders carefully, and for a long time.

How to behave on the slopes

It doesn't matter how good you are — you have to know and respect the basic rules of snowboarding. When you are surfing on a trail with other snowboarders and skiers, it is essential to show good sense and follow certain rules of behavior. These are rules that have been carefully thought-out so that a carefree day on the snow does not turn into a bad memory.

• Always respect others
Every rider must always be respectful of the other people on the trails (including skiers) as far as speed and conduct are concerned. Do not act in such a way as to endanger others.

• Respect nature
When you are riding off-trail, be careful not to trample over small trees and do not disturb the fauna in the woods.
Do not pollute by throwing your trash away, but bring it down to the valley — and do a good turn by bringing down that left behind by the ill-bred.

• Control speed and trajectory
While riding, keep your speed within your limits and appropriate to the snow conditions, visibility, and number of people on the slopes. Don't change direction suddenly unless you have already checked to make sure that you have enough space around you.

• Pass with prudence
You can pass on the right or the left but you must leave the person you are passing enough space to continue his or her descent without having to make an abrupt change. If you're not sure, warn the person first.

• Reentering on the trail after a pause

Make sure that no one is coming down the trail before you reenter after having made a stop.

NOVICE RIDER

ADVANCED RIDER

FREESTYLE CARVING RIDER

• Respect the signals

Always respect the warnings and signs posted along the trails. Do not go down trails that have been closed. Don't use trails that have been carefully prepared for races — you will ruin them.

• Always carry identification

Any rider who has been in or has witnessed an accident should be able to show personal identification.

• Safety leash

It is advisable to be tied to the board with a safety leash. A board that falls from a chairlift or slides uncontrolled down a trail can kill somebody.

• Don't stop in the middle of the trail

If you have to make a stop, even a short one, don't do it in the middle of the trail. It's better to stop on the side so as not to bother anyone. Don't stop where there is poor visibility, or behind a hill, or in a narrow place after a curve.

• Ascents and descents on foot

If, for some reason, you have to detach the board and walk, don't do so in the middle of the trail. Walk on the outside of the trail so as not to hinder others.

• Always give the right of way

Whoever comes from behind must always give the right of way to the person in front.

• It's your duty to help others

Helping others in case of an accident is not only an obligation, it is right and proper.

Avalanches

Heat and cold, sudden temperature changes, and the wind all change the conditions of snow. The most dangerous slopes are those with slopes between 25° and 35°. It takes only one rider to make a layer of unstable snow come loose. High-risk zones include places where snow has been stacked up by the wind, and slopes under crests, gullies, and hollows. When you're near a dangerous area, undo your safety leash, slip one strap of your backpack off, so you'll be able to drop it immediately if necessary, and proceed in single file, keeping a good, safe distance between you and other riders. Avoid crossing the slope horizontally; head instead down the steepest decline. Think of possible escape routes. If there is no chance of an escape to the side, try to surf the snow in movements that are as long as possible. Try to ride on the surface and not let yourself get sucked into the snow. Keep your nose and mouth free; many people use neoprene bands or a scarf to cover them. If you find yourself under the snow, don't start digging your way out randomly; instead, try to figure out where the surface is. The simplest way to figure out which direction is "down" is by spitting; then proceed in the opposite direction. Try to remain calm. Don't waste your energy or slow down your breathing. If you witness an avalanche, notify the ski patrol immediately and place a guard there to take note of any landslides. The rescuers' detectors must be set to the "receive" position; any search will be in vain if just one rescuer has it on the transmitting position. These may all seem obvious or easy, but in a panic, the first thing you lose is the ability to think clearly.

CLASSIFICATION OF AVALANCHES

	CRITERION	CHARACTERISTICS AND DESIGNATION	
DETACHMENT ZONE	START OF DETACHMENT	From a point: weak cohesion avalanche	From a fracture line: avalanche of large slabs
	SURFACE POSITION OF SLIPPAGE	Within snow mantle: surface avalanche	Between snow mantle and ground: deep avalanche
	WETNESS	Dry snow: dry snow avalanche	Wet snow: wet snow avalanche
SLIDE ZONE	SHAPE OF THE SLOPE	Flat: slope avalanche	Gully: gully avalanche
	TYPE OF MOVEMENT	Turbulent: cloud form avalanche	Slide along the slope: skimming avalanche
ACCUMULATION ZONE	GRANULOMETRY OF ACCUMULATED SNOW	Coarse: large deposit	Fine: fine deposit
	WETNESS OF DEPOSIT	Dry: deposit of dry snow	Wet: deposit of wet snow
	PRESENCE OF DEBRIS	Absent: clean deposit	Present: deposit with debris (stones, earth, trees and branches)

Fakie and more

Every freestyler knows that you can have a good time even if there is no half-pipe or snow park around. There is a whole series of tricks, some still being developed, that can satisfy any rider. And practicing tricks will increase your confidence and lead to a faster technical evolution.

ONE FOOT

It was the legendary Shaun Palmer who tried this impressive trick for the first time. Ride with your front leg hooked onto the board and your back leg free, placed in front of the binding. The trick consists of a backside air with your free foot projected in the opposite direction from the one on the board. Landing is very tricky; the board must be kept under control so that your free foot can come down on the deck and you can get your balance back. This trick is very dangerous, not to be attempted by the inexperienced.

FAKIE-RIDING

Snowboarding backwards. This move is essential, especially for freestylers. Your setup is important: the less the bindings face the nose, the easier it will be to guide the board backwards. Start off by riding some diagonals, first forward, then backwards. Shift your weight alternately from your front to your back leg, and try to execute mirror movements. In order to turn fakie, think about the first turns you ever made and repeat the steps: from bending to straightening up to gradually switching edges. Correct distribution of your body weight is important — it should not be too far back. When you're able to control your fakie riding, you'll be ready to try your first ollies. Knowing how to ride fakie is also important for spinning tricks.

SWITCHSTANCE

Another term for riding fakie.

WHEELIE

Tricks balanced on the nose or tail of the board. Start from a relaxed position, bending the leg that you want to keep in contact with the snow, and take your weight off the other end of the board. It will lift up automatically. Help this along by stretching your arms and body upwards. When your arms are in a sideways position, they'll help you regain your balance.

Ollies and jumps

The ollie is the basic move that opens all freestyle doors. An ollie is a jump made without the help of ramps. This jump and its name come from skate-

boarding. Jumping without a ramp might seem difficult. But it's only a matter of learning how to use the elasticity of the snowboard.

DOING AN OLLIE WITH STYLE

As you start, bend your knees and bring your body weight onto your rear leg. Straighten up quickly and bring your front leg up to your chest. The unloaded nose of the board will follow, lifting up from the snow. At this point, use the elasticity of the board by bringing your weight to the center, and let the tail come up from the snow, helped by your bent rear leg. Bring your arms up as you straighten up. Once you're in the air, bring your legs up to your body and stay in a crouched position to keep flying. Get ready to land by straightening your legs; absorb the impact by bending them.

Half-pipe

Before entering the half-pipe, the best playground for freestylers, you must master all the freeriding techniques.

Experience in straight jumps, especially on steep slopes, helps, as do dry runs on a trampoline.

your legs bent; keep your center of gravity low and in the middle of the board. Attack the pipe wall at a vertical angle, unless it is very low and soft. Bend your front leg more than your back one.

BASIC HALF-PIPE TECHNIQUE
In the beginning, it's much more important to learn the basic technique than to do a lot of tricks.
You should be able to ride across the pipe, forward or fakie. You have to be able to ride the walls without slowing down.

Aerials – as well as reentry – must be done without hesitation.
The time spent acquiring these fundamental skills will be rapidly repaid because you will learn the more difficult tricks much more quickly.
Try to enter the pipe with

Keep your center of gravity centered on the board. Beginners can get air by pushing forcefully against the wall.

Expert riders gain speed from the landing and crossing and fly above the rim without pushing too much.

Stiffy

An expression for "straight leg." In this trick, your legs are completely straight as you grab hold of the frontside edge with your forward arm. This is a classic freestyle trick; it gives the impression that you're standing still in the air for a second, frozen at the apex of a parabola traced by the board. This trick is done primarily in the half-pipe.

Approach the ramp or wall in a crouched position and at a constant speed (1). Anticipate the jump by straightening up. This will launch you higher (2-3). Stay centered on the board in order to keep it under control.

Bend your legs, grab the frontside edge with your forward hand, and prepare to straighten your legs (4). Now you are at the apex of the trajectory, and can do a Stiffy. Try to straighten your legs completely (5).

Hold the position for as long as you can. Prepare to land. Let go of the edge (6), bring the board under your body, keeping it under control (7), and straighten your legs as if you wanted to flatten the board on the ground (8).

When you hit the snow, absorb the impact by bending your legs and keeping your weight centered on the board (9).

Nose-bone

"Bone" denotes tricks done by extending one leg while bringing the other up to the body. The tricks have different names depending on which leg is extended: Nose-bone when the front leg is extended, Tail-bone when it's the back leg. In the beginning, extending your limbs in an unnatural way and staying in a stalled position for so long will make you assume unnatural positions. Try to come out of the pipe by applying equal pressure to both your legs. As you are about to land, straighten your bent leg and bend the other so that you will be in the right position to absorb the impact. Since this involves an exaggerated extension of your legs, it's important to prepare by stretching.

Three different ways of approaching a Nose-bone: with a frontside grab (above) and a backside one (right). Other variations are a frontside grab with the forward hand and a tail-grab with the back hand. There are also more complex composite tricks like the Tai-Pan, which consists of a frontside grab between the legs with the forward hand.

Tail-grab

In skateboard and snowboard jargon, a "grab" is any trick in which your hand holds onto the board. All grabs are made in the air, with or without spinning around, even if one trick involves a backside turn with the back hand grabbing the frontside edge. Grabs can be done with one or two hands and also with hands crossed in different positions on the board. A tail-grab is when the tail of the board is held; there are several tricks that include this grab. In the beginning, choose a small mound and practice jumping as high as you can, so you'll have enough time to do the trick. Stay centered on the board, at least in your first attempts. Bring the board close to your body while bending your legs, then reach back to make the grab.

The simplest variation is grabbing the frontside edge with the back hand, close to the nose.

The natural finish of a tail-grab is to combine it with a Nose-bone.

Backside air

The backside air, a direct descendant of the backscratcher, has, like the method air, managed to carve out its own space, not only because it is a basic half-pipe trick, but because it is also a spectacular one. In competitions, judges always give high scores when this trick goes high and is well executed. Although it may resemble a method air

at first sight, it differs from it in two ways. The first is the grab: here, the front hand grabs the backside edge near the nose of the board. The second is the position of the rear leg: here, it is extended so that the board is at an oblique angle to the jump.

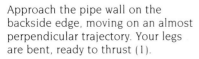

❶

Approach the pipe wall on the backside edge, moving on an almost perpendicular trajectory. Your legs are bent, ready to thrust (1).

❷

Your knees are close for better stability, your weight centered on the board. Your eyes are on the pipe rim (2).

❸

Support the jump by straightening your legs and body with power, helping yourself if necessary by moving your arms (3).

The first times you approach the pipe it will be difficult to keep your movements balanced so you don't land outside of the pipe or in the middle of it (4). Right after you jump, bend your legs in order to control your movement and grab the backside edge (5).

It is important to keep your board under control, to make sure it is always under your body, and to keep your eyes on the point along the wall where you want to land (6-7).

At the highest point of the jump, when you feel that the stalling phase has finished, begin straightening out to get ready to land (8-9), cushioning your impact.

Just before you come down on the pipe wall, take your hand off the backside edge as your legs bring the board back under your body. Reenter along the steep part of the pipe, where the slope is greatest, so you can approach the opposite wall at maximum speed (10-11).

Method air

When snowboarding began, the only jump imaginable was the backscratcher, a name borrowed from freestyle skiing. It was done by bending the legs backwards so the heels came close to the buttocks, then grabbing the board with the forward hand near the binding. A lot of time has passed since then but the backscratcher and its successor, the method air, are still the tricks everyone learns first. They are also important in helping you learn other freestyle tricks. The method air has more style than its predecessors, due to a different arching of the body. When correctly executed, the method air is one of the most beautiful tricks.

A high, long method air like this one, executed by the Swiss Reto Lamm, although not as spectacular as rotations or corkscrews, is still a very elegant trick. For some, it symbolizes freestyle snowboarding.

The sequence here was executed on a quarter-pipe, but it is possible to do it on a trail by taking advantage of natural differences in heights. Approach the steepest slope in a crouched position at moderate speed (1), ready to straighten up and push yourself up above the lip (2-3).

Crouch and grab the backside edge with your front hand (4). At the apex of the parabola, as you stall, arch your body with your rear arm stretched out (5).

Prepare for landing by bringing the board up under your body and rotating it in the direction of your exit (6-7-8).

540° (five-forty)

If you want to make more than one complete rotation in the air, the secret is to jump as high as possible, pushing your legs to their limits at the moment of the launch. Anticipate and follow the rotation of the board by rotating your head and shoulders completely, and bring up your legs once you're in the air to accelerate your movement. Always keep your landing point in sight. All rotation tricks can be personalized by adding grabs, bones, and slowing them down.

You can think about finishing a 540° on both sides of the pipe by approaching them forward or in fakie. Remember that with this trick, as with a 180° but unlike a 360°, you will land in the same direction you took off in.

If you go up the wall fakie, you'll be in fakie when you reenter. Speed is important for the success of this trick, even if a slower and higher rotation is more spectacular. So it's essential that your head and shoulders give impetus to the movement of your upper body, and then to your legs (1-2-3-4). If your legs are bent close to your body, they will increase the speed of rotation. As soon as you begin to come down, keep your eyes on your landing point, which should stop the rest of your body from rotating (5-6). Straighten out your legs as you head toward the pipe wall (7-8), and get ready to lower your center of gravity as you land, to get your balance back, pick up speed, and head towards the opposite wall so you can start the next trick.

Half-pipe tricks

The half-pipe offers infinite possibilities for creative tricks. During the last few years, the easiest tricks have evolved into elaborate ones and now border on the spectacular. These are the principal tricks, which have become part of snowboard culture.

AIR
Aerial tricks performed above the pipe rim.
- **AIR IN FAKIE**
Landing and crossing the pipe backwards.
- **BACKSIDE AIR**
Mirrors a frontside air, performed on the backside edge.
- **FRONTSIDE AIR**
Airs performed on the frontside edge.

GRAB
Aerial tricks where the board is grasped by the hand. All grabs may be done frontside and backside.
- **INDY**
The frontside edge is grabbed with the rear hand, usually in front of the rear binding.
- **INDY NOSE-BONE**
The front leg is extended, the rear one bent. The frontside edge is grabbed with the rear hand.
- **LIEN AIR**
The backside edge is grabbed with the rear hand, with the body bent backwards toward the backside edge.
- **MELLONCH OLLIE**
The backside edge is grabbed with the front hand, the front leg is extended (Nose-bone).
- **MELLOW**
The backside edge is grabbed with the front hand, usually between the bindings.
- **METHOD AIR**
The backside edge is grabbed with the front hand, usually between the bindings. The front leg bends as the rear leg extends.
- **MUTE AIR**
The frontside edge is grabbed with the front hand, usually between the bindings.
- **NOSE-BONE**
The front leg is extended while the back leg bends.
- **NOSE-GRAB**
The nose of the board is grabbed with the front hand.
- **STALE FISH**
The backside edge is grabbed behind the body with the back hand, the back leg is extended.
- **STIFFY**
The frontside edge is grabbed and both legs are extended parallel to the ground.

- **TAIL-GRAB**
The back hand grabs the tail of the board.
- **TWEAK**
A body spin during an air.

ROTATIONS
- **BACKSIDE**
A backward kick and a 360° fakie rotation.
- **CABALLERIAL**
Taking off frontside with a forward rotation.
- **FRONTSIDE**
Taking off backside with a backward rotation.
- **SWITCHSTANCE 360°**
A switchstance take-off followed by a forward 360° rotation.

FLIPS WITH ROTATIONS
- **CORKSCREW**
Rotations executed at an angle, not perpendicular to the ground.
- **540° CORKSCREW**
Backside jump with a 540° rotation and a fakie landing.
- **HAAKON FLIP**
Named after its inventor, the legendary champion Terje Haakonsen, this 720° fakie backflip approaches the wall backwards. The body does a 720° rotation while executing a backward somersault.
- **MCTWIST**
Forward jump and a 540° rotation.

TOPSY-TURVIES
Flips carried out by placing one or both hands on the rim of the pipe.
- **ELGUERIAL**
The wall is approached in a fakie, the back hand braces itself for a somersault while the front hand grabs the backside edge.
- **MILLER FLIP**
The front hand braces itself for a somersault while the back hand grabs the frontside edge.

How to build a jump

Fig. A

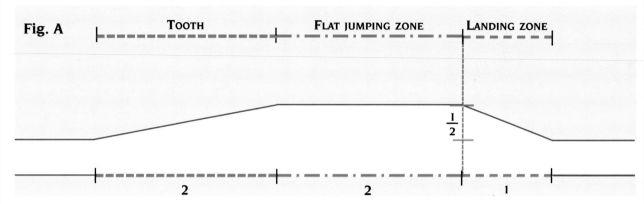

TOOTH	FLAT JUMPING ZONE	LANDING ZONE
2	2	1

The numbers on figure A indicate the proportions;
figure B is a graphic representation of the final result.

Fig. B

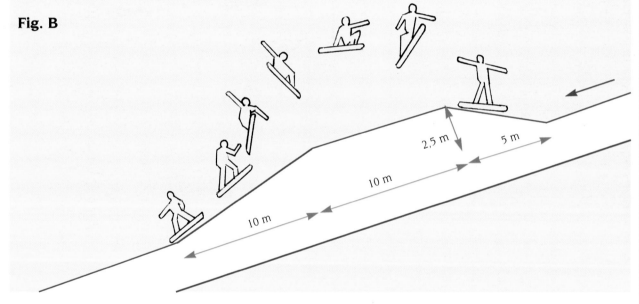

It is not difficult to build a small jump in snow.
The space required is available on almost any trail
and the amount of snow that has to be moved is not
enormous. Nor will it be hard to find other freestylers
who will be willing to help you. Be sure, though, to
always get permission from those responsible for the
trail. They will be able to direct you to less trafficked,
safer places with the correct slope and enough space for
running and landing. A shovel and some elbow grease
can work miracles. The essential ingredient, however,
is compact, crystalline snow. The proportions and
dimensions of your jump must be appropriate to your
own ability. Building a jump that's too difficult will lead
to accidents. Proceed by degrees; it can always be raised

and lengthened. Practice your speed. If your approach
is too slow, you won't make it over the jump.
On the other hand, if your approach is too fast,
you may land beyond the landing slope. The shape
of the take-off point – its angle, length, and curve – is
very important for doing tricks well, and depends
on the rider's ability and the type of trick he's doing.
For example, a rodeo or a misty flip requires a greater
thrust. The landing zone should not be flat, but rather
slope slightly, to avoid getting caught in a trap.
Start with the easier tricks, like straight jumps
(for example, tail-grabs), then go on to rotations
like the 180° as you gain confidence. Then you can
experiment with more complicated tricks.

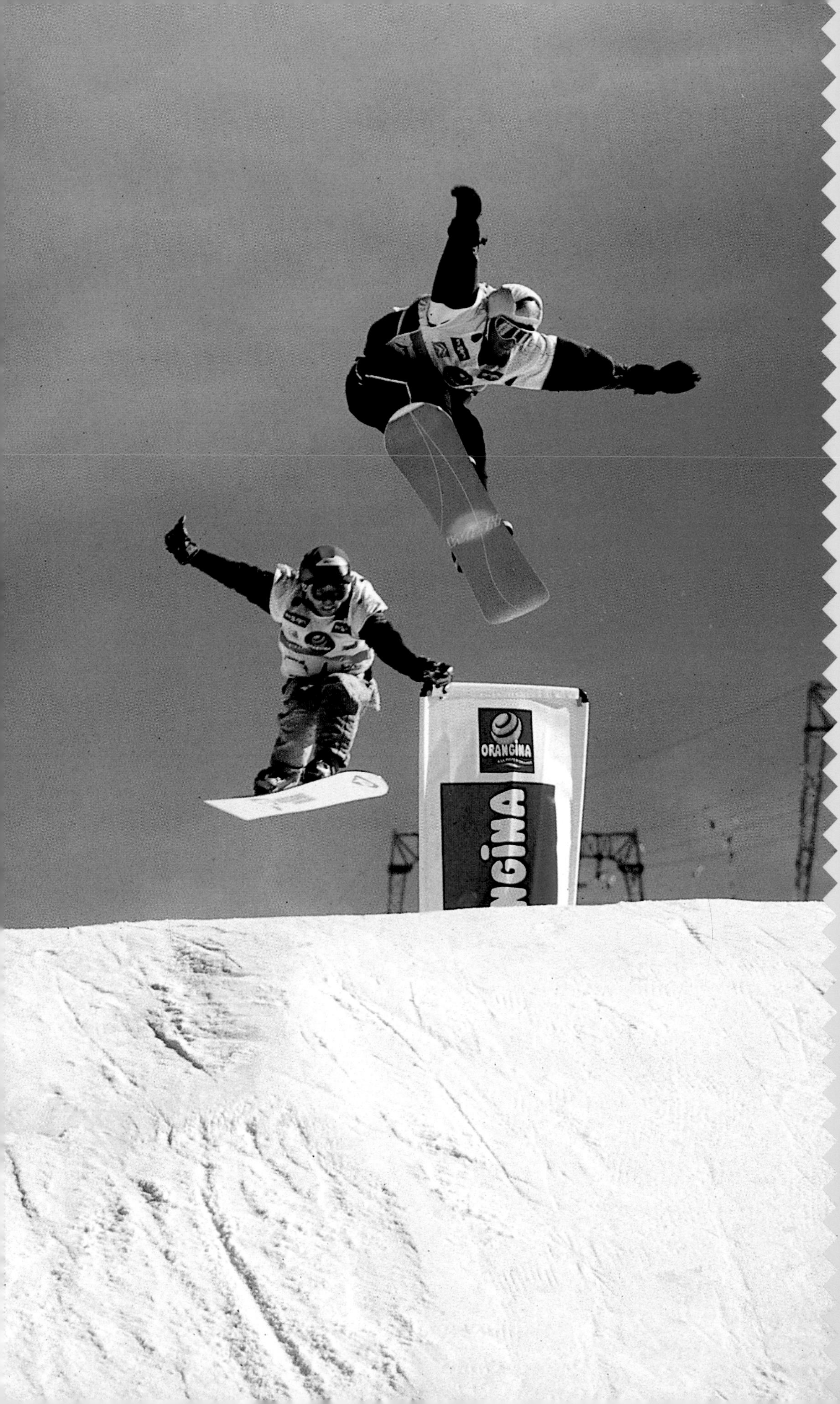

BOARDERCROSS

Boardercross

Boardercross, also known as "boarder" and abbreviated BX, is a discipline designed to satisfy both hard riders and soft ones. It was originally known as the Derby and involved a group start down a slope without gates or a defined course as the Banked Slalom, with long turns and small jumps, though riders started one at a time.

THE TRACK

Examine the track carefully to figure out which lines are the best.

BOARDERCROSS ADVICE STARTING TACTICS

Concentrate. Study your opponents in order to decide whether to attack immediately, so you're ahead at the first obstacle, or whether it's better to adopt a defensive strategy and attack during the run. Lean your board against the starting gate; you'll gain a second or two.

HOW TO HANDLE THE TURNS

If you don't feel at ease on these banked turns, you can choose to keep a high trajectory so as to run on a flat board. It's important to keep your speed constant, and to not grip the edge too much.

WHOOPS

Whoops are a series of jumps, so it's important to check out the distance between them and their height. This way you'll be able to decide whether to jump them or absorb them. Don't move your upper body — let your legs do all the work.

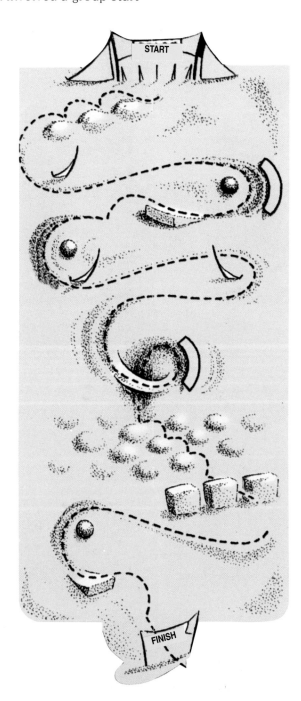

HOW TO HANDLE THE JUMPS

Keep your balance, even in flight. Stay crouched and then straighten up, extending your legs as you land. Try to stay as close as possible to the ground. Keep the board flat.

RACES

Today, boardercross usually involves four riders starting at the same time from a gate. There are exceptions: in the X-Games in the U.S., six riders start; in a super-boardercross, ten start at once. Runs last from 30 seconds to a minute. They include single or double jumps, "whoops" (moguls), long curves, and obstacles like bottlenecks, traffic islands, and tunnels. Riders do race against the clock, but when there are many participants only the first two finishers advance. Starting order is determined by drawing lots as well as standing in international and national series. Boardercross is not particularly dangerous, but it does require a helmet and other protection, since so many riders participate at once. Boardercross is

EQUIPMENT

A helmet is indispensable (especially one designed for boardercross). Other protective equipment is also recommended, like that used in Motocross: chest guards, back guards, knee pads, and elbow pads. While some racers prefer casual attire, others opt for fitted or slalom suits. The choice is yours; there is no official outfit.

becoming more and more popular, and it is bound to succeed even more. It is a race based on physical contact like motocross, from which it has borrowed a great deal. Passes are often made in turns and on jumps; riders try to make their opponents lose their balance. Boardercross has the competitive spirit of parallel slalom and the creativity of freeriding.

Banked turns

You can pass your opponents in turns more than anywhere else. That's why you must practice a lot, trying out high lines (close to the rim), low ones (close to the base), and middle ones. You'll learn how the board reacts, and how much space you need for the different paths. After you try them out on your own, practice with other riders so you get used to the chaotic conditions of a race.

1

2

3

4

5

6

7

Remember that your greatest ally is speed. By exploiting centrifugal force, you'll stay glued to the turn and keep your action fluid.

If you choose a high trajectory, you will go farther but you won't slow down. If you choose a low path, you'll gain some distance but lose speed. Make your decision in response to your opponents' behavior.

Whether you approach the turn frontside (1-12) or backside (13-17), the secret is to maintain a position in which your body is perpendicular to the ground and the board is flat. A crouched position will guarantee stability (14-17).

Your eyes should always be on your next obstacle (5-6-7, 15-16-17), but never lose sight of your opponents. If you have a good technique but a slight build, concentrate on the smoothness of your style, which will help you gain speed.

Snowboard camps

AUSTRALIA

- **SNOWAVE SNOWBOARD CAMP**
Australia, Thredbo,
Perisher Blue (Jindabyne)
Mt. Buller
Hotham (VIC)
Phone: 61-2-9977-7488
Fax: 61-2-9977-1289
Address: 46 Pittwater Rd.
Manly - 2065 Sydney
e-mail:
snowave@ozemail.com.au

AUSTRIA

- **BILLABONG KILLER CAMP**
Sölden
Phone and Fax:
43-222-310 1317
Address: Billabong Killer
Camp Stroheckgasse 2/6
A-1090 Vienna
- **SPC SKATE 'N
SNOWBOARD SUMMER CAMPS**
Hintertux Glacier
Phone: 43-664-30-80-547
Fax: 43-5285-2205
Address: Sporthotel Strasse
A - 6290 Mayerhofen

CANADA

- **CAMP OF CHAMPIONS**
Blackcomb Mountain,
Whistler
Season: June - July
Phone: 604-938-3450
Fax: 604-938-9582
Address: 2713 Sproat Dr.,
Whistler, B.C. VON 1B2
Web Site: http: //www.
campofchampions.com
- **CRAIG KELLY'S WORLD
SNOWBOARD CAMP**
Blackcomb Mountain
Phone and Fax:
360-599-1258
Address: P.O. Box 5090,
Glacier
Washington 98244
- **HIGH CASCADE
SNOWBOARD CAMP**
Whistler
Phone: 604-938-3450
Fax: 604-938-9582

Address: 2713 Sproat Dr.
Whistler, B.C. VON 1B2
Web Site: http:
//campofchampions.com

FRANCE

- **FREESTYLER CAMP**
Tignes
Phone: 33-45-066 5171
Fax: 33-45-066 5175
Address: 37, rue Central
74940 Annecy le Vieux
- **DEEP ICE SNOWBOARD
CAMP**
Les 2 Alpes
Season: June - July - August
Phone: 39-546-642193
Fax: 39-546-642193
Address: Sportiga
Via S. Mamante 126
Faenza (RA) - Italia
- **NAZCA SNOWBOARD
CAMP**
Tignes: June-August
Les 2 Alpes:
July - September
Phone: 39-165-31322
Fax: 39-165-97680
Address:
Nazca Snowboard Club
Via Paravera, 6
11100 Aosta
e-mail: nazca@netsurf.it
Web Site:
http://nazca.netsurf.it
- **DINO BONELLI CAMP**
Les 2 Alpes
Season: June - September
Phone: 39-174-553187
33-476-790501
Fax: 39-174-555630

JAPAN

- **JEFF FULTON'S
SNOWBOARD CAMP**
Tougaike Resort Hakuba
Nagano-Ken
Season: March - April
Phone: 81-261-72-7888
Fax: 81-261-72-4175
Address:
6334 Hokujo Kita-Azumi
Hakuba Nagano-Ken
Japan 399-93

ITALY

- **BIG A SUMMER CAMP**
Val Senales (BZ)
Season: July
Phone: 39-347-2231529
Fax: 39-125-751882
Address: Via Iervis 76,
10015 Ivrea (TO)
Web Site:
http://www4.iol.it/big.a
- **BURTON SNOWBOARD CAMP**
Stelvio (SO)
Season: June.- August
Phone: 39-464-519597
Fax: 39-464-510283
Address: Sport Agency
via S. Caterina, 94/L
Arco (TN)
e-mail:
burtonagency@anthesi.com

NORWAY

- **THE SNOW CO. CAMP
FOLGEFONN**
Phone and Fax: 47-6-759-1599
Address: The Snow Co.
P.O. Box 24
1330 Oslo Lufthavn
- **SNOWBOARD CAMP STRYN**
Stryn
Phone: 47-2-269-3030
Fax: 47-2-269-9440
Address: Snowboard Norge AS
P.O. Box 5395
Majorstua N-0304 Oslo

UNITED STATES

- **WINDELL'S SNOWBOARD
CAMP**
Mt. Hood, OR
Season: June
Fax: 503-622-4582
Address: P.O. Box 628,
Welches, OR 97067
e-mail:
windcamp@teleport.com
Web Site:
http://www.highcascade.com
- **MOUNT HOOD SNOWBOARD
CAMP**
Mt. Hood, OR
Phone: 503-688 8322
Fax: 503-668 7986

Address: 17140 Fir Drive
Sandy, OR 97085
e-mail: mhsc@aracnet.com
Web Site:
http://www.aracnet.com/
mhsc/
- **ROCKY MOUNTAIN
SNOWBOARD CAMP**
Winter Park, CO
Phone and Fax: 970-879-9059
Address: P.O. Box 1148
Steamboat Springs,
CO 80488
- **UNITED STATES
SNOWBOARD TRAINING
CENTER**
Mt. Hood, OR
Season: June - August
Phone: 503-622-4430
Fax: 503-622-3337
Address: P.O. Box 360
Brightwood, OR 97011
- **BOARDERLINE SUMMER
SNOWBOARD CAMP**
Mt. Alyeska, AK
Phone: 907-349-9931
Fax: 907-333-0832
Address: 800 E. Diamond
Blvd. #171
Anchorage, AK 99515

SWITZERLAND

- **FLAG SNOWBOARD
FREERIDE CAMP**
Pontresina
Season: June - July
Phone: 41-1-450-74-76
Fax: 41-1-450-74-75
Address: P.O. Box 1123
8038 Zurich
e-mail:
mflag@access.ch
- **ICE RIPPER CAMP**
Saas-Fee
Phone: 41-1-291-0440
Fax: 41-1-261-2801
Address: Ice Ripper Camp '97
CH - 8026 Zurich
- **JAME'S B FRUITASTIC
SNOWBOARD CAMP**
Les Diablerets
Season: June
Phone and Fax: 41-21-784-4041
Jame's B Organisation Rte.
Du Jorat 39a
1000 Lausanne 27

Racing specialties

Parallel slalom

Competitors descend two at a time next to each other on parallel trails, one red, the other blue. The thirty-two finalists are judged on their total time. An elimination to sixteen is made, always by the best total time from two trails. In case of a tie, there is a head-to-head run.

Giant slalom

This race consists of one run. If there are a lot of competitors, there is an initial qualification before the final. In general, fifty men and thirty women start. If there are two runs, the starting order is inverted for the first 16 men and the first 8 women.

Slalom

One of the most spectacular events, the special slalom is won on the basis of seconds and hundredths of seconds. What counts most of all is the rapidity of movement; great agility is required to shift edges as fast as possible, along with skill in choosing the fastest lines. Here, too, the race consists of two runs.

Half-pipe

The original freestyle event, inspired by skateboarding competitions not only because of the tricks executed but also because of the half-pipe structure. The riders compete with airs and other tricks in two qualifying rounds; the sixteen best go on to the finals. The number of tricks, style, height, and landings are taken into account in the scoring. The jury is made up of five judges and a chief judge.

Protection

In alpine races, protection is important to reduce the impact of gate poles. Helmets are essential, although some racers prefer lighter, softer models with integrated chin guards and head protection.

Thanks to technical advances, racers are hitting the trails faster and faster, and protective equipment has become more refined. In really fast races, it is also necessary to wear back protection.

The slalom is not particularly fast; danger is more likely to come from contact with the poles. Both snowboarders and skiers use the same protection: a helmet to protect their faces and shin guards and padding for their arms, often as an integral part of their suits. In giant slalom, the internal poles at the gates are smaller, so riders can lean over more without the risk of banging into the hard plastic poles. Many racers choose to wear only a helmet in this event, to be more aerodynamic.

Slalom technique

Acceleration when exiting a turn

When watching alpine snowboard races, you can see the different ways of handling changes of direction and exit techniques, or rather, speed when exiting a turn. These techniques can be divided into two categories: high exoneration and pendulum exoneration. Both are effective, but the first is best for beginners. It is also preferable on courses with gates placed far from one another. When the gates are close to each other, though, or when there are deep ruts or the speeds are high, more experienced riders will opt for the pendulum exoneration, which is a little more difficult.

HIGH EXONERATION
The rider applies strong pressure to the board by an accentuated bending of the knee. Just as he changes edge, he makes an extension that unloads the board and quickly switches to the opposite edge (right). He loads the edge again, bending his legs once more.

PENDULUM EXONERATION
The legs move like a pendulum under the upper body, which remains still. The legs have the job of loading and accelerating the board, pushing the side down when they are bent. In order to change edge, the knees are drawn up close to the body, then extended and pushed as he exits the turn. Proper distribution of body weight is essential: it must be on the forward leg when entering the turn, on the back leg when exiting.

Giant slalom technique

This is the most popular alpine event, but certainly not the easiest. Like alpine skiing, it requires great preparation, both technical and physical, since you're moving faster than in the slalom (which requires greater agility and coordination). It's a bit like comparing the 400-meter and 100-meter events in track and field. In order to do well in the giant slalom, it's important to refine your sensitivity and smoothness so you can better "read" the slope and anticipate the turns. Handling turns and choosing lines are the most important things. Slalom techniques for accelerating out of turns may also be used in the giant slalom, although some riders think they're unnecessary and may be harmful to perfecting one's technique and effective action between the poles.

FRONTSIDE TURN
With a good angle inside the turn, the body can lean at an incredible angle (thanks also to the short inside gate pole) and take turns at high speeds. Your eyes should always be on the next pole, to anticipate switching edges and the line through the turn.

BACKSIDE TURN
The photo at right demonstrates a perfect hip angle: because of body structure, the backside stance limits the possibility of absorbing irregularities in the trail. The rider is bent low, not only to load the board and guide it through the curve with precision, but also because this is the most efficient aerodynamically. The rider's arms are spread out for better balance.

THE ANGLE

The angle of the body helps the edge grip better in turns. In frontside turns, the upper body remains bent while it leans towards the inside of the turn (opposite top). In backside turns, a good angle is obtained by pushing the hip towards the inside of the turn while the upper body is bent forward and towards the outside (this page, and opposite bottom). It's harder to correct errors in backside turns, so choose a fairly safe line.

Training techniques and methods

Now that you've seen the different alpine disciplines, the time has come to think about the kinds of training necessary for the different races. Each race, in fact, requires different approaches and tactics. The best way to train is to get used to different trails. Alpine snowboard courses are very similar to those for skiers, but unlike skiers, snowboarders move on only one edge so it is very difficult to recover from errors. When you train, try to re-create as wide a range of trajectories as possible.

Angled trajectory

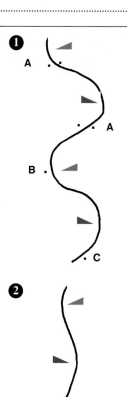

Start on an angled trajectory, on a trail with an average slope.
In the beginning, it will be useful to place markers that will act as signals to make the necessary move at the right point:
(A) start to change edge,
(B) greatest slope,
(C) end of turn.
Get used to keeping a continuous speed from the very beginning.

Fast run

Now try a fast run by decreasing the angle of the gates.
Training on stretches with a slight slope will give you time to check the position of your body and the grip of your edges, as well as improve your talents at speed.

Angled run 1

An angled run is laid out on a slight slope.
This will let you perfect your technique in order to reduce friction to the minimum.

Angled run 2

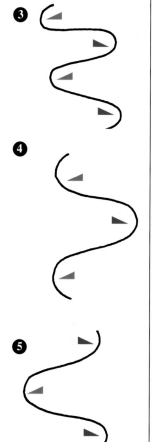

Increase the difficulty by moving to a steeper slope and laying out a run with the gates closer together. This will let you improve your performance, especially in changing edges quickly. Edge changes must be fast and, at the same time, there must be a greater angle in guiding the board.

Finishing the progression

Finish the progression by keeping the angled layout but increasing the space between the gates, to concentrate again on increasing your speed.

THE "COMBS"

The "combs" are a different training method. The poles are placed very close to one another with hardly any angle so that they are in a line. This will improve your coordination and edge-changing speed. The line of poles can be placed on the steepest slope, or to your individual needs. The principal layouts are as follows:

MEDIUM SLOPE

A) The poles are at a slight angle and placed at regular intervals. This run helps establish a rhythmic pace.

B) Increase the angle at which the poles are placed but keep the distance between them regular. This run breaks up the rhythm.

C) The run develops along a diagonal that can follow the slope to the right or to the left. It helps to decrease the slope.

D) At certain points, the poles are placed closer together or further apart. This helps break up the rhythm.

STEEP SLOPE

A) The poles are at angles but placed at regular intervals. This helps improve control at high speeds.

B) The angle of the gates increases while the distance between the poles decreases. This helps improve reaction time.

C) The angle of the poles decreases as does the distance between them. This course is faster.

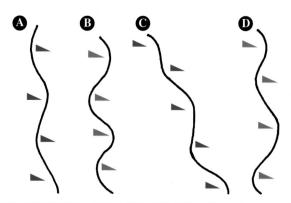

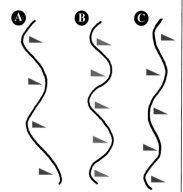

Snow spots of the world

COUNTRY	REGION	PLACE	ALTITUDE (METERS)	LIFTS	TRAILS (KMS)
AUSTRIA	ARLBERG	Lech-Zurs - Tel. 43-5583-2245	1450-2500	88	200
	CARINTHYA	Bad Kleinkirchheim - Tel. 43-4240-8212	860-2250	32	85
	SALZBURG	Altenmarkt Zauchensee - Tel. 43-6452-5511	1800-2700	65	150
		Badgastein - Tel. 43-6434-2531	1070-2055	36	250
		Saalbach Hinterglemm - Tel. 43-6541-7272	1010-2100	59	180
	STYRIA	Schladming - Tel. 43-3687-22268	750-2700	78	140
	TYROL	Kitzbuhel - Tel. 43-5356-2272	800-2000	66	158
		Ischgl - Tel. 43-5444-6561	1400-2860	72	200
		Mayrhofen - Tel. 43-5285-2305	700-2250	30	90
		Neustift - Stubaital - Tel. 43-5226-2228	1000-3200	83	100
		St. Anton - Tel. 43-5446-22690	1300-2800	80	260
	VORALBERG	Schruns Montafon - Tel. 43-5556-72166	700-2370	73	200
CANADA	ALBERTA	Banff - Lake Louise - Tel. 403-522-3555	1700-2700	12	55
		Mount Norquay - Tel. 403-762-4421	1640-2200	9	53
		Sunshine Village - Tel. 403-762-6500	1658-2730	12	78
	BRITISH COLUMBIA	Blackcomb Mountain - Tel. 604-687-1032	670-2300	15	90
		Panorama - Tel. 604-342-6941	540-2000	14	60
		Whistler Mountain - Tel. 604-685-1007	660-2200	17	80
	QUEBEC	Mont Saint Anne - Tel. 418-827-4561	200-1100	12	60
FRANCE	MARITIMES ALPS	Auron - Tel. 33-4-93230266	1600-2450	26	130
		Avoriaz - Tel. 33-4-50740211	1800-2700	250	650
		Isola 2000 - Tel. 33-4-93231515	2000-2650	23	120
		La Meje - Tel. 33-4-92247188	1350-2800	76	250
	HAUTE SAVOY	Chamonix Mt. Blanc - Tel. 33-4-50532400	1035-3850	62	160
		Flaine - Tel. 33-4-50908001	1650-2500	80	260
		La Clusaz - Tel. 33-4-50026092	1100-2600	58	130
		Les Contamines Montjoie - Tel. 33-4-50470158	1164-2450	34	80
		Megève - Tel. 33-4-50212728	1115-2350	82	300
		Portes du Soleil - Tel. 33-4-50733254	800-2350	224	650
		Saint Gervais - Tel. 33-4-50477608	850-2350	82	300
	ISÈRE	Alpe D' Huez - Tel. 33-4-76803473	1860-3330	82	220
		Les 2 Alpes - Tel. 33-4-76792200	1650-3600	85	220
	HAUTES ALPES	Briançon - Serre Chevalier - Tel. 33-4-92247188	1350-2800	76	250
	SAVOY	La Plagne - Tel. 33-4-79097979	1850-2650	28	100
		Les Arcs - Tel. 33-4-79071257	1250-3250	113	210
		Les 3 Vallées Courchevel - Tel. 33-4-79080029	1600-3200	81	150
		Tignes - Tel. 33-4-79065671	1100-3300	193	600
		Val d' Isère - Tel. 33-4-79060660	2100-3600	101	300
		Val Thorens - Tel. 33-4-79000808	1790-3600	50	120
			2800-3200	48	80
SWITZERLAND	VALAIS	Crans Montana - Tel. 41-27-412132	1484-3000	42	160
		Grachen St.Niklaus - Tel. 41-28-571457	1617-2920	13	40
		Saas-Fee -Tel. 41-28-571457	1800-3600	42	145
		Verbier - Tel. 41-26-316222	1500-3330	99	400
		Zermatt - Tel. 41-28-661181	1620-3820	73	230
	VAUD	Leysin - Tel. 41-25-342244	1270-2300	74	200
		Les Diablerets - Tel. 41-25-531358	1200-3000	74	200
		Villars - Tel. 41-25-353232	1300-2217	74	200
	GRISONS	Bri Gels - Tel. 41-81-9411331	1100-2500	11	50
		Davos - Tel. 41-81-4152121	1560-2844	58	315
		Flims - Laax - Tel. 41-81-9214343	1020-3018	32	220
		Piz Mundaun Obersaxen - Tel. 41-81-9331515	1250-2285	20	120
		San Bernardino - Tel. 41-91-8321767	1600-2525	9	40
		Savognin - Tel. 41-81-742222	1210-2700	18	80
		Scuol - Tel. 41-81-8649494	1480-2220	15	80
		Splugen - Tel. 41-81-621332	1244-2800	9	35
		St. Moritz - Tel. 41-82-33147	1856-3100	60	350
	BERNESE ALPS	Adelboden - La Lenk - Tel. 41-33-738080	356-2400	51	166
		Gstaad - Saanenland - Tel. 41-30-88181	1100-3000	69	250
	JUNGFRAU	Grindelwald - Tel. 41-36-531212	1034-3450	45	200
		Meiringen - Hasliberg - Tel. 41-36-713922	1230-2450	15	60
		Murren - Tel. 41-36-568686	1650-2970	17	50
		Wengen - Tel. 41-36-551414	1150-2500	19	100
	CENTRAL SWITZERLAND	Andermatt - Tel. 41-44-67454	1450-2970	13	56
		Engelberg - Tel. 41-41-941161	1050-3020	26	50
	EAST SWITZERLAND	Braunwald - Tel. 41-58-841108	1400-1900	8	30
		Toggenbourg - Tel. 41-74-52727	894-2260	20	50

Vail (Colorado)

With its beautiful scenery, mountain lakes, and nature, Vail, Colorado, is a unique and popular place for snow lovers.

TOURIST OFFICE OF VAIL VALLEY
P.O.Box 309
Vail, CO 81658
Phone: 800-525-3875
970-476-1000
Fax: 970-476-6008
Web Site: www.vail.net
*e-mail:*webmaster@vail.net

Vail is an enchanting spot in the Rocky Mountains about 90 miles from Denver. Situated in a delightful natural setting, it is surrounded by small towns reminiscent of the pioneer days. The best way to enjoy this stupendous landscape is to rent a car and drive around. The climate is dry and never too cold. Snowfall is generally abundant, the snow dry and powdery, ideal for backcountry riding. The resort does have artificial snow equipment. The many trails, equipped with ultramodern lifts, can satisfy the needs of any snowboarder. But snowboarding is not the only attraction Vail offers its guests. There is all kinds of recreation, from ice hockey to gyms and fitness centers furnished with the latest equipment. And for shoppers, there is a choice of stores ranging from the most luxurious to the most specialized. A lively nightlife is guaranteed by a variety of discos and night clubs. Vail is at 8,000 feet; the lifts take you up to 11,300 feet. The 21 lifts carry some 35,820 people per hour to 120 trails: 32% for beginners, 36% for intermediate snowboarders, and 32% for experts.

Banff National Park (Canada)

Banff National Park, in southwestern Canada in the province of Alberta, 78 miles from Calgary, is the oldest park in Canada. Created in 1885 on 10 square miles, it has since expanded to 2,564 square miles. This growth was due both to the intrinsic qualities of the region and to the enterprise of its early inhabitants. There are two stupendous ski areas inside the park: Mount Norquay and Sunshine Village. Both are close to the town of Banff, famous for its hydrothermal springs and magnificent scenery. Zoning laws protect the town, limiting the number of inhabitants to 7,000. So one has all the pleasures of a peaceful little town as well as every imaginable service. The strict legislation that regulates the life and development of the park ensures that nature is protected. It's not unusual to run into a family of caribou grazing calmly on somebody's lawn. The Mount Norquay resort, a paradise for riders who love to carve, has a great snow park with a half-pipe, an immense table-top, and a quarter-pipe that seems to touch the sky. The snow park has artificial snowmaking equipment, so the snow is usually hard enough. The trails are always very smooth, but there are also some excellent spots for freeriding. The resort is owned by the Grandi family, whose son, Thomas, is one of the top World Cup alpine skiers as well as an excellent snowboarder. Sunshine Village, about 12 miles from Banff, can be reached by a cable-car several miles long that connects all the lifts. There is no artificial snow at Sunshine Village because there is no need for it. Every cloud brings soft, dry powder. Even the well-used trails have a powdery surface, which most riders prefer to hard. Cliffs, trees, and canyons abound, offering something for all levels of riders. Sunshine Village has been classified by *Snow Country* magazine as the best resort in the Canadian Rockies and the thirteenth best among North American ski resorts. It took fourth place for the quality of its snow, which averages 24.5" to 40" a year.

BANFF MOUNT NORQUAY
Phone: 403-762-4421
Fax: 403-762-8133
Web site:
www.banffnorquay.com
Web Site: www.skibanff.com
e-mail: info@banffnorquay.com
BANFF SPRINGS HOTEL
from 4:00 p.m. to 7:00 p.m.
Phone: 403-762-3771
UNLIMITED SNOWBOARD SCHOOL
Phone: 403-762-8208

Banff National Park is paradise for riders, with abundant new snow throughout the year, enchanting views, and world-famous athletes who go there to train.

Lake Louise (Canada)

The Lake Louise ski resort is about thirty miles west of Banff, on the Trans-Canada Highway. Set in a magnificent valley, the town has just a few houses, services, and several hotels. The quality of the snow is superb; if it doesn't satisfy a rider on a certain day, rain checks are offered. *Ski* magazine ranks it fifth among North American resorts. Lake Louise has a number of very impressive trails and lifts in four different areas: the front side/south face, the back bowls, Larch area, and Ptarmigan/Paradise. It also boasts of a wide selection of skis and snowboards for rental, which should satisfy even the most picky skiers, while an excellent ski school runs numerous courses for all levels throughout the season. Situated at the foot of the Victoria Glacier, this splendid resort is a natural mecca for mountainbiking, jogging, and dogsledding as well as the perfect place in summer for kayaking.

CHATEAU LAKE LOUISE
from 3:00 p.m. to 8:00 p.m.
Phone: 403-522-3511
**LAKE LOUISE
MOUNTAIN OFFICE**
Phone: 403-522-3555
SKI SCHOOL
Phone: 403-522-1333
Web Site:
www.skilouise.com
e-mail:
vertical@skilouise.com

Lake Louise's location guarantees excellent snow throughout the winter.

The trails at Lake Louise have been designed to satisfy the needs of all riders, from beginners to champions.

Even though the trails are usually well-prepared, it is possible to strike out on new powder among pine trees.

Panorama B.C. (Canada)

Panorama is in the heart of the Rocky Mountains, about four hours by bus from Calgary in British Columbia. This is one of the capitals of heli-skiing, which has become popular with those who like to reach inaccessible places with really great snow. This is obviously an expensive indulgence, requiring special transportation, equipment, and highly skilled guides. R.K. Heli-Skiing is one of the local companies that offers this service. But R.K. has received special access from the government, and is able to guarantee skiing on virgin snow at all times. Twelve-seater helicopters are usually used; each group is accompanied by a qualified guide. The day starts early, with a briefing on safety rules. The sternness of each guide is equaled by his kindness. Discipline is obligatory in this sport: potential danger is always present. Any behavior that might jeopardize the safety of the rider or any one else is not tolerated. The helicopter makes descents of about six miles possible on slopes of varying difficulty.

Panorama offers not only spotless slopes and fresh snow every day, but also an excellent heli-skiing service to reach inaccessible places, where the snow is always perfect.

WOAITO
Phone: 604-342-6941
Fax: 604-342-3395
Web Site:www.panoramaresort.com
SCHOOL OF SKIING AND SNOWBOARDING
Box 66, Invermere, BC, VOA 1K0
Booking: 1-888-SOS-7799
e-mail: info@skischool.com

Les 2 Alpes (France)

At Les 2 Alpes, it's possible to snow-board in incomparable off-trail areas on the largest glacier in Europe from June to October, from dawn to dusk. Located in the Oisans Massif, Les 2 Alpes is a veritable paradise for winter sports. In fact, it's considered one of the best areas in France for both summer and winter sports. For the past seven years, at the end of each October, it has hosted the "Mondial du Snowboard." This "Woodstock of Snow" opens the winter season, attracting national and international champions and a large number of snowboard fans.

With its splendid glacier, the Les 2 Alpes resort offers an unending season to all riders.

LES 2 ALPES
BP 7 - 38860 Les 2 Alpes
Phone: 33-4-76792200
Fax: 33-4-76790138
Web Site:
www.les2alpes.com
e-mail: Les2Alp@icor.fr

SUMMER SNOW

Les 2 Alpes, with the biggest and highest glacier in Europe, is the European capital of summer snowboarding:
- 500 acres of trails;
- 8,400 to 11,000 feet altitude, 2,400 feet vertical drop;
- 20 lifts, 2 automatic coupler gondolas, 1 funicular, 3 chairlifts, and 6 skilifts, 2 automatic coupler chairlifts, 1 gondola, 1 cable car, 2 skilifts for children;
- 1 permanent snow park, half-pipe, Module contest, Boardercross.

NATURE

Marked trails, protected nature, shelters, and traditional villages. This and much else are available for those who love sports at this mountain, with its 12,000-foot peaks: Ecrins, Meije, and Pelvoux.

SNOWBOARDING

You can be sure of snow, sun, and fun at Les 2 Alpes. For the last seven years this resort has organized the "Mondial du Snowboard" at the end of October for "snow surfers." It also has one of the best snow parks in Europe, as well as boardercross, a half-pipe, module contest, and a summer camp.

In addition to its splendid views, the resort offers a wide variety of sports for the young and the not so young.

Even after snowboarding there is no lack of sports activities, from freeclimbing to mountain-biking, sailing, and rollerblading.

Ruka (Finland)

The little Finnish village of Ruka is only twelve miles from the Russian border, just under the Arctic Circle. Ruka has become known worldwide thanks to the Junior World Championship. Every year, more than 300 young snowboarders from more than thirty countries come together for four days. Ruka is the cradle of the world's best snowboarding talents. Every one of them enjoys total freedom and independence in the far north. Some go berserk in their search for speed as they adventure out on the flat desert of Finnish snow, or fly down steep slopes with their mini-toboggans. It's not surprising that all the reindeer seem to go on vacation during the Junior World Championship.

MATKAILUKESKUS KARHUNTASSU
Torangintaival 2,
93600 Kuusamo FL
Phone: 358-8-85020910
Fax: 358-8-8502901
e-mail: ktassu@.kuusamo.fi

The peacefulness of nature and the silence of uncontaminated, solitary landscapes provide a backdrop for magical Ruka.

Innsbruck (Austria)

The most difficult half-pipe race in the Alps takes place every year during the winter season on the Nordkette, 3,600 feet above Innsbruck. This is a bittersweet cocktail of fun, tough races, and even tougher time conditions.

Thanks to the location, the wonderful atmosphere, and a really difficult half-pipe, this race is considered the most important of the season. It's up to the crowd to judge the big tricks and rotations that push the limits of safety. The twenty-two top snowboarders in the world offer their best here, as they cavort like Tasmanian devils in an effort to win.

A few minutes from Innsbruck, at Axamer Lizum, riders can find whatever they need in the way of snowboard equipment.

At Christmas every year, one of the most famous snowboard competitions is held in the Bergisel Stadium – the Air & Style Snowboard Contest – where riders from all over the world come to perform their breathtaking jumps for more than 25,000 spectators.

TOURISMUS VERBAND
Burggraben 3,
A-6020 Innsbruck
Phone: 43-512-59850
Fax: 43-512-598507
Web Site:
www.tiscover.com/innsbruck
e-mail:
info@innsbruck.tvb.co.at

Saas-Fee (Switzerland)

Saas-Fee, the village of glaciers, sits at 5,400 feet at the foot of the Dom, the highest Swiss mountain, surrounded by thirteen of the highest peaks in the Alps. It was already a famous ski resort in the nineteenth century; tourists continue to go to the first hotel, built in 1883, even though it means climbing to it on foot or riding on the back of a mule. Saas-Fee has one of the most extensive ski networks in the Alps, with forty-eight miles of winter trails and twelve miles of summer ones. Skiing and snowboarding at Saas-Fee are seasonless, and skiers and snowboarders can find trails suitable for all levels. Saas-Fee is also famous for the Alpine Express train and the Alpine Metro, the highest subterranean funicular in the world, which goes from 9,000 to 10,500 feet in two and a half minutes underneath the Felskinn rock to the Mittelallalin. The alpine school at Saas-Fee also organizes unforgettable excursions to the glaciers and the region's highest peaks.

SUMMER TRAILS
Twelve miles of easy and difficult trails, open from 7:30 a.m. to 2:00 p.m.
A 240-foot half-pipe and a "fun-box" are dedicated to snowboard racing teams.

TOURIST OFFICE SAAS-FEE
CH - 3906 Saas-Fee
Phone: 41-28-571457
Fax: 41-28-571860
Booking:
Phone: 41-28-591120
e-mail: to@saas-fee.ch

WINTER TRAILS

Sixty miles of trails, 25 intermediate and 25 expert. Two 240-foot half-pipes for the fearless and a snowboard "fun-box." Saas-Fee is well-equipped with lifts: 2 gondolas, 8 skilifts, 2 chairlifts, 3 cable-cars, plus the famous Alpine Metro and 13 Alpine Express cable-cars, which can carry more than 25,000 people per hour.

Zermatt (Switzerland)

Zermatt is a kingdom of winter sports, with Mt. Matterhorn, the mountain's mountain, always looming in the background. Zermatt is one of the most fascinating – and still untouched – winter resorts in the Alps. The village still has its original appearance: there are no cars in Zermatt, it can be reached only by train. And there is not only snow; some 18 miles of mountain trails make it a stupendous place to live year-round.

In this magnificent setting snowboarding has found an uncontaminated landscape.

This is the sunniest ski resort in the Alps; thanks to its southern exposure, it is protected from the winds, yet always sure to have snow. It has more than 70 lifts, including cable-cars, and skilifts divided among three areas. Its trails, from the easiest to the most difficult, provide 138 miles of descents.

TOURIST OFFICE OF ZERMATT
CH - 3920 Zermatt
Phone: 41-28-661181
Fax: 41-28-661185
Web Site: www.zermatt.ch
e-mail: zermatt@wallis.ch
SKI SCHOOL
Phone: 41-28-675444
Fax: 41-28-675189

Madonna di Campiglio (Italy)

Whether it is snowboarding for fun or snowboarding for competition, this part of the Italian Alps is perfect. Madonna di Campiglio hosts a unique sports organization that ranges from alpine skiing to snowboarding, from the yearly Snowboard World Cup to the special slalom races of the World Cup 3-Tre, one of the most important international races. Recognized by the Snowboard Federation as one of the most important snowboarding areas, the "Pearl of the Brenta" has events and well-groomed trails year-round. Situated in the heart of the Brenta Dolomites at the foot of Mount Adamello, Madonna di Campiglio promises fun and thrills on the "Direttissima Spinale," one of the most famous trails in Europe, a fantastic expert trail for those who love the steepest slopes. The "Amazzonia-Alta" trail has an average slope of 40%, is about 900 to 1200 feet wide, and almost a mile long. If this isn't enough, there is an extensive network of 30 lifts, 90 miles of downhill trails, and 18 miles of cross-country. Best of all, there are no lines to stand on as one chooses between downhill, cross-country, backcountry, alpine skiing, telemark, and snowboarding.

**TOURIST OFFICE
MADONNA DI CAMPIGLIO -
PINZOLO - VAL RENDENA**
Phone: 39-465-442000
Fax: 39-465-440404
Web Site:
www.aptcampiglio.tn.it
e-mail:
aptcampiglio@well.it

Snow-white peaks challenge the sky while snowboarders circle in the December sun. Only the best compete. Snow is guaranteed, as are trails for all levels, and lifts without lines. Madonna di Campiglio offers this and a lot more to snow lovers.

Snow spots in the U.S.

ALASKA
- **EAGLECREST SKI AREA**
155 South Seward St.
Juneau
Phone: 907-790-20000
Fax: 907-586-5677
Web Site:
www.ptialaska.net/~cbjhelp/ea
glcrst.htm
Peak Elevation (feet): 2600
Number of Trails: 31
Number of Lifts: 3
Snowboard Park, Half-Pipe
Season: Nov 22 - Apr 19

CALIFORNIA
- **KIRKWOOD**
P.O. Box 1
Kirkwood
Phone: 209-258-6000
Web Site:
www.aminews.com/kirkwood
Peak Elevation (feet): 9800
Number of Trails: 65
Number of Lifts: 12
Snowboard Park
Season: Nov - May
- **MAMMOTH MOUNTAIN**
P.O. Box 24
Mammoth Lakes
Toll-Free Phone: 800-228-4947
Main Phone: 760-934-2571
Fax: 760-934-0603
Web Site:
www.rsn.com/~mammoth
Peak Elevation (feet): 8200
Number of Trails: 30
Number of Lifts: 7
Snowboard Park
Season: Dec - Apr
- **NORTHSTAR AT TAHOE**
P.O. Box 129
Hwy 267 & Northstar Dr
Truckee
Toll-Free Phone: 800-466-6784
Main Phone: 530-562-1010
Fax: 530-562-2215
Web Site:
www.aminews.com/northstar
Peak Elevation (feet): 8610
Number of Trails: 63
Number of Lifts: 12
Snowboard Park, Half-Pipe
Season: Nov - Apr
- **SKI SIERRA AT TAHOE**
1111 Sierra-at-Tahoe
Twin Bridges
Phone: 530-659-7453
Fax: 530-525-4170
Web Site: www.sierratahoe.com
Peak Elevation (feet): 8852
Number of Trails: 44
Number of Lifts: 10
Snowboard Park
Season: Dec - Apr

- **SNOW VALLEY SKI RESORT**
P.O. Box 2337
Running Springs
Phone: 909-867-2751
Fax: 909-867-7687
Web Site:
www.aminews.com/snowvalley
Peak Elevation (feet): 7898
Number of Trails: 37
Number of Lifts: 13
Snowboard Park, Half-Pipe
Season: Nov - Apr
- **SUGAR BOWL SKI RESORT**
P.O. Box 5
Norden
Phone: 530-426-9000
Fax: 530-426-3723
Web Site:
www.aminews.com/sugarbowl/
Peak Elevation (feet): 8383
Number of Trails: 80
Number of Lifts: 12
Snowboard Park, Half-Pipe
Season: Nov - May

- **TAHOE DONNER ASSOCIATION - LAKE TAHOE**
11509 Northwoods Blvd
Truckee
Phone: 530-587-9444
Fax: 530-587-9419
Web Site:
www.aminews.com/tahoedon
ner
Peak Elevation (feet): 7350
Number of Trails: 12
Number of Lifts: 3
Snowboard Park, Half-Pipe
Season: Dec 15 - Apr 4

COLORADO
- **BRECKENRIDGE SKI AREA**
1599 Summit Country Rd 3
P.O. Box 1058
Breckenridge
Toll-Free Phone: 800-789-7669
Main Phone: 970-453-5000
Fax: 970-453-3260
Web Site:
www.aminews.com/northstar
Peak Elevation (feet): 12998
Number of Trails: 126
Number of Lifts: 20
Snowboard Park, Half-Pipe
Season: Oct - May
- **CRESTED BUTTE MOUNTAIN RESORT**
P.O. Box A
Crested Butte
Toll-Free Phone: 800-544-8448
Main Phone: 970-349-2333
Fax: 970-349-2208
Web Site:
www.cbinteractive.com/cbws

Peak Elevation (feet): 12162
Number of Trails: 85
Number of Lifts: 13
Snowboard Park, Half-Pipe
Season: Nov 21 - 19 Apr
- **VAIL**
P.O. Box 7
Vail
Toll-Free Phone: 800-525-2257
Main Phone: 970-476-9090
Fax: 970-845-5745
Web Site: vail.net
Peak Elevation (feet): 11450
Number of Trails: 121
Number of Lifts: 26
Snowboard Park, Half-Pipe
Season: Nov 8 - Apr 20
- **WINTER PARK RESORT**
P.O. Box 36
Winter Park
Toll-Free Phone: 800-979-0332
Main Phone: 303-726-5514
Fax: 303-453-5823
Web Site:
www.skiwinterpark.com
Peak Elevation (feet): 12060
Number of Trails: 121
Number of Lifts: 20
Snowboard Park, Half-Pipe
Season: Nov - Apr

MICHIGAN
- **BOYNE HIGHLANDS**
P.O. Box 19
600 Highland Rd
Harbor Springs
Toll-Free Phone: 800-462-6963
Main Phone: 616-549-6030
Web Site: www.boyne.com
Peak Elevation (feet): 1100
Number of Trails: 42
Number of Lifts: 9
Snowboard Park, Half-Pipe
Season: Nov - Apr
- **BOYNE MOUNTAIN**
P.O. Box 19
1 Boyne Mountain Rd
Boyne Falls
Toll-Free Phone: 800-GO-BOYNE
Main Phone: 616-549-6030
Fax: 616-549-6094
Web Site: www.boyne.com
Peak Elevation (feet): 1220
Number of Trails: 41
Number of Lifts: 10
Snowboard Park, Half-Pipe
Season: Nov - Apr

MINNESOTA
- **AFTON ALPS**
P.O. Box 129
6600 Peller Ave So.
Hastings
Toll-Free Phone: 800-328-1328

Main Phone: 612-436-5245
Fax: 612-436-8584
Number of Trails: 38
Number of Lifts: 18
Snowboard Park, Half-Pipe
Season: Nov - Apr
- **GIANT'S RIDGE**
P.O. Box 190
Biwabik
Toll-Free Phone: 800-688-7669
Fax: 218-865-4733
Number of Trails: 34
Number of Lifts: 6
Half-Pipe
Season: Nov - Apr
- **WELCH VILLAGE**
P.O. Box 146
Welch
Toll-Free Phone: 800-421-0699
Main Phone: 612-258-4567
Fax: 612-222-2813
Web Site:
www.aminews.com/welch
Peak Elevation (feet): 1005
Number of Trails: 36
Number of Lifts: 9
Snowboard Park, Half-Pipe
Season: Nov - Mar

MONTANA
- **BIG SKY SKI AND SUMMER RESORT**
P.O. Box 160001
Big Sky
Toll-Free Phone: 800-548-4486
Main Phone: 406-995-5000
Fax: 406-995-5001
Web Site:
ww.mv.com/biz/tiworks/bigski
Peak Elevation (feet): 11166
Number of Trails: 75
Number of Lifts: 15
Half-Pipe
Season: Nov - Apr
- **RED LODGE MOUNTAIN**
P.O. Box 750
Red Lodge
Phone: 406-446-2610
Fax: 406-446-3604
Peak Elevation (feet): 9416
Number of Trails: 69
Number of Lifts: 8
Snowboard Park
Season: Nov 15 - Apr 12
- **SHOWDOWN SKI AREA**
P.O. Box 92
Neihart
Toll-Free Phone: 800-433-0022
Main Phone: 406-236-5522
Fax: 406-236-5523
Peak Elevation (feet): 8200
Number of Trails: 34
Number of Lifts: 4
Snowboard Park, Half-Pipe
Season: Dec - Apr

NEVADA

• DIAMOND PEAK
1210 Ski Way
Incline Village
Phone: 702-832-1177
Web Site:
www.aminews.com/diamond
Peak Elevation (feet): 8540
Number of Trails: 30
Number of Lifts: 7

• HEAVENLY
P.O. Box 2180
Stateline
Toll-Free Phone: 800-2-HEAVEN
Main Phone: 702-586-7000
Web Site: www.skiheavenly.com
Peak Elevation (feet): 10100
Number of Trails: 79
Number of Lifts: 25
Season: Nov - Apr

NEW HAMPSHIRE

• LOON MOUNTAIN SKI AREA
RR#1 Box 41
Kancamagus Hwy
Lincoln
Phone: 603-745-8111
Web Site:
www.mainstream.com/~loon
Peak Elevation (feet): 3050
Number of Trails: 43
Number of Lifts: 8
Snowboard Park
Season: Nov - Mar

NORTH CAROLINA

• SUGAR MOUNTAIN RESORT
P.O. Box 369
Banner Elk
Toll-Free Phone: 800-784-2768
Main Phone: 704-898-4521
Fax: 704-898-6820
Web Site:
www.aminews.com/sugarmt
Peak Elevation (feet): 5300
Number of Trails: 18
Number of Lifts: 8
Snowboard Park
Season: Nov - Mar

OREGON

• MOUNT BACHELOR
P.O. Box 1031
Bend
Toll-Free Phone: 800-829-2442
Main Phone: 541-382-2442
Fax: 541-382-2442
Web Site:
www.aminews.com/mtbachelor
Peak Elevation (feet): 9065
Number of Trails: 70
Number of Lifts: 11
Snowboard Park, Half-Pipe
Season: Nov - Jul

• MOUNT HOOD MEADOWS SKI RESORT
1975 SW 1st Ave-Suite M
Highway 35
Mt. Hood
Toll-Free Phone: 800-SKIHOOD
Main Phone: 503-337-2222

Fax: 503-227-7693
Peak Elevation (feet): 7300
Number of Trails: 82
Number of Lifts: 11
Snowboard Park, Half-Pipe
Season: Nov - May

• TIMBERLINE SKI AREA
Timberline Lodge
Toll-Free Phone: 800-547-1406
Main Phone: 503-272-3311
Fax: 503-272-3710
Web Site:
www.teleport.com/~timlodge
Peak Elevation (feet): 8540
Number of Trails: 30
Number of Lifts: 6
Snowboard Park, Half-Pipe
Season: Sep 27 - Sep 7

PENNSYLVANIA

• JACK FROST
P.O. Box 703
Hwy 267 & Northstar Dr
Blakeslee
Toll-Free Phone: 800-475-SNOW
Main Phone: 717-443-8425
Fax: 717-443-0780
Peak Elevation (feet): 2000
Number of Trails: 21
Number of Lifts: 7
Snowboard Park, Half-Pipe
Season: Dec - Mar

• SEVEN SPRINGS
RD#1
P.O. Box 110
Champion
Toll-Free Phone: 800-452-2223
Main Phone: 814-352-7777
Fax: 814-352-7911
Web Site:
www.aminews.com/sevensprings
Peak Elevation (feet): 2990
Number of Trails: 30
Number of Lifts: 18
Snowboard Park, Half-Pipe
Season: Dec - Apr

• WHITETAIL SKI RESORT
13805 Blairs Valley Rd.
Mercersburg
Phone: 717-328-9400
Web Site:
www.aminews.com/whitetail
Peak Elevation (feet): 1800
Number of Trails: 17
Number of Lifts: 6
Snowboard Park, Half-Pipe
Season: Dec - Apr

UTAH

• PARK CITY MOUNTAIN RESORT
P.O. Box 39
Park City
Phone: 801-649-8111
Fax: 801-647-5374
Peak Elevation (feet): 10000
Number of Trails: 89
Number of Lifts: 14
Season: Nov - Apr

• BRIAN HEAD RESERVATION CTR
P.O. Box 190008
356 S Highway 143
Brian Head

Toll-Free Phone: 800-272-7426
Main Phone: 801-677-2042
Web Site:
www.aminews.com/brianhead
Peak Elevation (feet): 11307
Number of Trails: 53
Number of Lifts: 6
Snowboard Park, Half-Pipe
Season: Nov - May

• SNOWBIRD SKI & SUMMER RESORT
P.O. Box 929000
Salt Lake City
Toll-Free Phone: 800-453-3000
Main Phone: 801-742-2222
Fax: 801-742-3344
Peak Elevation (feet): 1100
Number of Trails: 66
Number of Lifts: 9
Snowboard Park
Season: Nov - May

VERMONT

• KILLINGTON-PICO
P.O. Box 129
400 Killington Rd.
Killington
Toll-Free Phone: 800-621-6867
Fax: 802-422-4391
Web Site: www.killington.com
Peak Elevation (feet): 4170
Number of Trails: 212
Number of Lifts: 33
Snowboard Park, Half-Pipe
Season: Oct - Jun

• MOUNT SNOW/HAYSTACK
Mountain Rd.
West Dover
Toll-Free Phone: 800-245-7669
Main Phone: 802-464-3333
Fax: 802-464-4135
Web Site:
www.mountsnow.com
Peak Elevation (feet): 3600
Number of Trails: 130
Number of Lifts: 24
Snowboard Park, Half-Pipe
Season: Nov - Apr

• OKEMO MOUNTAIN RESORT
R.F.D. #1
Ludlow
Phone: 802-228-4041
Web Site:
www.aminews.com/okemo
Peak Elevation (feet): 3344
Number of Trails: 85
Number of Lifts: 12
Snowboard Park, Half-Pipe
Season: Nov - Apr

• STOWE MOUNTAIN RESORT
Mt. Mansfield Co. Inc.
5781 Mountain Rd.
Stowe
Toll-Free Phone: 800-253-4SKI
Main Phone: 802-253-3000
Fax: 802-253-3406
Web Site: www.stowe.com/smr
Peak Elevation (feet): 4393
Number of Trails: 47
Number of Lifts: 11
Snowboard Park, Half-Pipe
Season: Nov - Apr

• STRATTON MOUNTAIN RESORT
RR 1 Box 145
Stratton Mountain
Toll-Free Phone: 800-STRATTO
Main Phone: 802-297-2200
Fax: 802-297-4300
Web Site:
www.genghis.com/stratton.htm
Peak Elevation (feet): 3875
Number of Trails: 90
Number of Lifts: 12
Snowboard Park, Half-Pipe
Season: Nov - Apr

WISCONSIN

• CASCADE MOUNTAIN
W10441 Cascade Mountain Rd.
Portage
Toll-Free Phone: 800-992-2754
Fax: 608-742-7899
Peak Elevation (feet): 1277
Number of Trails: 27
Number of Lifts: 8
Snowboard Park, Half-Pipe
Season: Nov - Mar

WYOMING

• JACKSON HOLE MOUNTAIN RESORT
P.O. Box 2618
Teton Village
Toll-Free Phone: 800-443-6931
Main Phone: 307-733-2292
Fax: 307-733-2660
Web Site:
www.jacksonhole.com/ski
Peak Elevation (feet): 10450
Number of Trails: 76
Number of Lifts: 10
Half-Pipe
Season: Dec 6 - Apr 12

• SNOWSHOE HOLLOW
P.O. Box 310
Afton
Phone: 307-886-9831
Web Site:
www.aminews.com/snowshoe
Number of Trails: 2
Number of Lifts: 1
Season: Dec - Mar

UNITED STATES SKI AND SNOWBOARD ASSOCIATION
Box 100
1500 Kearns Blvd
Park City UT 84060
Phone: 435-649-9090
Fax: 435-649-3613
e-mail: info@ussa.org
Web Site: www.usskiteam.com
www.ussnowboard.com

Glossary

- **AIR**
Any kind of jump executed on moguls or crests.
- **ALLROUND**
A board that is suitable for any use.
- **ALPINE**
The most popular style in Europe; chiefly on trails, using hard boots and asymmetrical boards.
- **ANTI-SLIP PAD**
Rubber layer on the board between the front and rear bindings which provides stability to the back leg on the ski lift.
- **ASSEMBLY ANGLE**
Degree of the angle at which bindings are attached.
- **ASYMMETRICALS**
Asymmetrically produced snowboards, with off-axis sidecuts; the deviation may vary depending on the type of construction. Asymmetrical boards are considered to be a specialized evolution in the technique of snowboard construction.

- **BACK-FLIP**
A backward loop.
- **BACKSIDE**
Any kind of maneuver or riding involving the heel edge.
- **BACKSIDE AIR**
Term used to define all half-pipe jumps that approach a wall on the backside edge.
- **BACKSIDE TURN**
Thrust executed and conducted on the backside edge.
- **BANKED SLALOM**
A slalom run with raised parabolic turns.
- **BASE**
The part of the board that comes in contact with the snow.

- **BONE**
Freestyle surfing style used in jumps, obtained by straightening one leg and bending the other.
- **BRIDGE**
See Prestressing.

- **CANTING WEDGE**
A plastic wedge that is placed under the front or rear binding in order to provide a more comfortable position for the snowboarder.
- **CARVING**
Extreme surfing style in turns without the skidding, conducted on the edge.
- **COPING**
The top rim of the half-pipe.

- **DOWNHILL**
Descent.
- **DROP-IN**
Departure order in the pipe.

- **EDGE**
Steel trim, continuous or segmented, forming a border around the inferior part of the snowboard.
- **EFFECTIVE EDGE**
The part of the edge that actually comes into contact with the snow.
- **EFFECTIVE EDGE LENGTH**
The length of the edge that actually touches the snow.

- **FAKIE**
Riding backwards.
- **FLAT**
The flat part of the pipe.
- **FLIP**
Looping.
- **FOAM SYSTEM**
Plastic foam construction used to make boards with foam cores.

- **FREESTYLE**
A term that includes all maneuvers, tricks, or jumps in the half-pipe and on the trail.
- **FRONTSIDE**
Any kind of riding or maneuvers executed on the toe edge of the board.
- **FRONTSIDE TURN**
See Backside turn.

- **GOOFY**
Riding with the right foot in front.
- **GRAB/GRABBING/GRIP**
Grasping the board during a jump.

- **HALF-PIPE**
A half-pipe of snow, usually created artificially. It is similar to a skateboard half-pipe and is used for freestyle tricks.
- **HARD-BOOTS**
Hard snowboard boots for plate bindings, made like ski boots.
- **HI-BACK/HIGH-BACK**
Soft binding spoiler.

- **KICK**
An "elevation" used to indicate the height of the nose and tail.
See Tail-kick and Nose-kick.
- **KIT**
All the necessary equipment for changing or preparing the board or part of the bindings.

- **LEASH**
Safety binding attached to the side of the front binding that fastens the snowboard to the rider.

- **LIP**
Superior border of a snow crest or of the half-pipe.
- **LOW KICK**
A shortened blade whose tip has a greater curve toward the top.

- **NOSE**
Front extremity of the board.
- **NOSE-GRAB**
Grasping the nose during a jump.
- **NOSE-KICK**
Raising the nose scoop.
- **NOSE-RIDE**
Riding on the nose of the board, executed by turning the back downhill and keeping the body almost parallel to the trail.
- **NOSE-TURN**
A turn executed on the nose.
- **NOSE-WHEELIE**
A short rearing up on the nose obtained by an extreme forward shift of the weight.

- **OFF THE LIP**
A surfboard term meaning a turn executed on the crest.
- **ONE-EIGHTY**
A 180° turn executed in half-pipe.

- **PLATE BINDING**
For hard boots, similar to cross-country ski bindings, but without a safety binding. This type of binding is preferred by Freestylers.
- **POWDER**
New snow.
- **PRESTRESSING**
The difference of height between the part touching the snow and the raised center of the board when it is flat on the ground.

- **PRO-JUMPS**
Artificial ramps used for mogul races or parallel slalom.
- **PUSHING**
Acceleration of the snowboard by using bending and straightening movements.

- **QUARTER-PIPE**
Half of a natural or artificial half-pipe.

- **RAMP**
An artificial or natural structure for jumps.
- **ROCKER**
Raising the tail: a "tail-kick".
- **ROUND-TAIL**
A tail with a rounded edge.
- **ROUNDED SQUARE-TAIL**
A straight tail with rounded corners.
- **RUNNING LENGTH**
See Effective edge length.

- **SANDWICH SYSTEM**
Construction technique for boards with cores in laminated wood and the upper strata in different materials.
- **SCOOP**
Raising the nose: Nose-kick.
- **SCRAPER**
Instrument used for removing excessive wax from the base of the board.
- **SHELL BINDING**
For soft boots, a plastic shell that holds the soft boot by means of a padded strap.
- **SIDECUT**
The difference between the widest and the narrowest points of the board.
- **SINTERED BASE**
Base whose structure is of an elevated molecular weight with special running features.

- **SNURFER**
Predecessor of the snowboard in the '60s, without bindings and edges, but with a leash to hold on to.
- **SOFT-BINDING**
Shell binding for soft boots: it consists of a plastic shell that holds the boot by means of a plastic strap.
- **SOFT BOOT**
Soft snowboard boot, suitable only for soft bindings.
- **SPIN**
Turn.
- **SQUARE-TAIL**
A straight tail with squared corners.
- **STANCE**
The distance between the centers of the front and rear bindings.
- **SWALLOW-TAIL**
A "V"-shaped tail, used in powder snow.

- **TAIL**
Rear extremity of the board.
- **TAIL-KICK/TAIL-LIFT**
Complete elevation of the tail.
- **TAIL-TURNS**
Making turns on the tail.
- **TAIL-WHEELIE/RIDE**
Raising of the tail by shifting body weight backwards; riding on the tail.
- **THREE-SIXTY**
A complete 360° turn executed on a trail or half-pipe; it also means a 360° turn executed on the edge.
- **TOE-EDGE**
Nose edge of the board (front edge).
- **TRANSITION**
Turn between the flat and vertical parts of the pipe.
- **TUNING**
Optimal preparation of the board.
- **TURN**
Push or thrust.

- **TWEAKED**
A complete spin of the body in the air during jumps in the pipe.
- **TWIST**
Rotation of the lower half of the body during a jump.

- **VERT**
The vertical part of the pipe.
- **VITELLI-TURN**
A dynamic thrust executed by leaning the body toward the inside of the curve as you make it. It is named after the Frenchman Serge Vitelli.

- **WALL-TRICK**
Also "Lip-trick": tricks carried out on the wall of the half-pipe.

Suggested reading

BOOKS

◆ SUSANNA HOWE
*Sick: A Cultural History
of Snowboarding*
St. Martin's Press, 1998

◆ KEVIN RYAN
*The Illustrated Guide to
Snowboarding*
Master Press, 1997

MAGAZINES

◆ *Blunt*
815 N. Nash
El Segundo, CA 90245
Phone: 310-640-7082
Subscriptions: 800-366-6670

◆ *Snowboarder*
33046 Calle Aviador
San Juan Capistrano,
CA 92675
Phone: 714-496-7849
Fax: 714-486-5922
e-mail:
SnwbrdrMag@aol.com

◆ *Snowboarding*
353 Airport Rd.
Oceanside, CA 92054
Phone: 619-722-7777
Fax: 619-722-0653
Subscriptions: 800-334-8152

◆ *Snowboard Life*
353 Airport Rd.
Oceanside, CA 92054
Fax: 760-722-0653
e-mail: sblife@twsnet.com
Web Site:
www.twsnow.com/html/
f_snowboard_life.html

◆ *Strength*
5050 Section Ave.
Cincinnati, OH 45212
Phone: 513-531-0202
Fax: 513-531-1421
e-mail:
email@strengthmag.com
Web Site:
www.strengthmag.com

◆ *TransWorld
Snowboarding Magazine
TransWorld Snowboarding
Business Warp*
TransWorld Publications
353 Airport Rd.
Oceanside, CA 92054
Phone: 619-722-7777
Fax: 619-722-0653

EDITOR: Cristina Sperandeo

TRANSLATION: Rhoda Billingslay

PHOTOS: Paolo Codeluppi, Massimiliano Angeli, Dino Bonelli, I.S.DF. Wojciech, Kuva-Tahko, John L. Kelly, Katja Delago, Colin Meagher, A. Hourmont, Florian Wagner, David Urban, Xandi Kreyzeder, Peter Rauch, Stefan Ruiz, Ace Kvale, O. Kunz, Affif Bellakoar, Rob Gracie, Gary Land, David Schenker, Timo Jarvinen, Andreas Rauter, Jeff Curtes, Vianney Tisseau, Trevor Graves, Mark Gallup, Jon Foster, Geoff Fosbrook, Richard Graves, Richard Walch, Jan Mackenzie, Calle Eriksson, Quinn Shields, Gunter Grobl.

COVER: Pentagram

Grateful acknowledgment for their invaluable assistance to Beppe Cargnino, technical expert for *Snowboard Magazine* and World Cup athlete, and Pierpaolo Pighini of *Snowboard Magazine*. Special thanks to Julia Fiechtner of Burton, and to Dino Bonelli (Snow King), Peter Bayir (I.S.F.), Petra Mussig, Dieter Krassnig, Christian Petrollini (T-Line), Burton, Snow Pro Bindings, Hot, Ray Ban, Sunshine, Northwave, Level, Nitro, Protective, Subwear, Fire & Ice, Nidecker.

The drawings and texts on page 50 are from the book "Stretching" by Giovanni Cianti, published by Sonzogno, Italy

LAYOUT: **CON**FUSIONE s.r.l.
PRODUCTION: Ready-made, Milan

First published in the United States of America in 1998
by UNIVERSE PUBLISHING
A Division of Rizzoli International Publication, Inc.
300 Park Avenue South
New York, NY 10010

© 1998 RCS Libri S.p.A.

All rights reserved. No part of this publication may be reproduced, stored in a retrieval system, or transmitted in any form or by any means, electronic, mechanical, photocopying, recording, or otherwise, without prior consent of the publishers

98 99 00 01 02 / 10 9 8 7 6 5 4 3 2 1

Printed in Italy

Library of Congress Catalog Card Number 98-61137

ISBN 0-7893-0222-5